PRAISE FOR

JULIA TURSHEN

SMALL VICTORIES

"This is Ms. Turshen's first cookbook as a solo author, but she has cowritten others with the likes of Gwyneth Paltrow and Dana Cowin. She's also a recipe tester and developer—a skill that shines through in a book aimed at aspiring, eager home cooks; you won't find any molecular gastronomy in these pages. Ms. Turshen is a self-deprecating, warm, and charming writer."

—*Wall Street Journal*

"Julia's book is like her—it's totally accessible."

—*Ina Garten*

"*Small Victories* is so lively, so encouraging, and so filled with easy solutions that it's the perfect book for someone who loves food but is nervous in the kitchen. I'll be giving it to every young cook I know."

—*Ruth Reichl*

"An inspiring addition to any kitchen bookshelf."

—*Real Simple*

"Rich in ideas, and far from basic in its span of recipes, this is a book that earns a place on any shelf."

—*Nigella Lawson*

"Julia's *Small Victories* is a HUGE VICTORY! It is the best cookbook ever; a stunning visual memoir that you'll soon have filled with Post-its and turned-down pages."

—*Sally Field*

NOW & AGAIN

"Turshen . . . is at the forefront of the new generation of authentic, approachable authors aiming to empower readers who might be newish to the kitchen."

—*New York Times*

"It's not just a book of gorgeous, thoughtfully curated menus for hosting a gathering. It's also an inspiring manifesto about how and why we cook today."

—*Eater*

"It's like having your best friend with you in the kitchen, if she happened to be a really, really good chef and teacher."

—*mindbodygreen*

"*Now & Again* is a kitchen essential tool."

—*Carla Hall*

"No one is better than Turshen at coming up with unpretentious, delicious, and approachable recipes for home cooks of varying skill levels. An essential purchase for circulating cookbook collections."

—*Library Journal Starred Review*

"Julia's personal stories, approachable recipes, and conversational tone suggest that you're sitting at her kitchen counter shelling peas or peeling carrots."

—*Vivian Howard*

"Julia invites us to broaden our tastebuds with her fresh, approachable, never-fussy cooking. *Now & Again* leaves no dish and no one behind. . . ."

—*Yotam Ottolenghi*

"Julia Turshen's new book is a rich compendium of recipes that are reassuringly doable, full of inviting flavor, designed to make life easier and bring pleasure to the kitchen as much as to the table. This would be quite enough, but added to this, Turshen elaborates on the recipes, adding advice as to how the various components of a recipe can be tweaked and turned into other dishes and—this is always a joy to the home cook—how leftovers can be refashioned into further meals."

—*Nigella Lawson*

FEED THE RESISTANCE

"What an incredible reminder of the power of food to bring people together. This book will inspire you, will make you want to talk, to listen, and to act. It will also make you very hungry."

—*Abbi Jacobson*

"Julia Turshen is my 'she-ro.' In *Feed the Resistance*, she gives us a manifesto for food activism."

—*Dr. Jessica B. Harris*

". . . empowering and inspiring anyone with a kitchen to help feed a movement."

—*Eater*

SIMPLY JULIA

ALSO BY JULIA TURSHEN (ME!)

Now & Again

Feed the Resistance

Small Victories

SIMPLY JULIA

110 EASY RECIPES FOR
HEALTHY COMFORT FOOD

JULIA TURSHEN

HARPER WAVE

An Imprint of HarperCollinsPublishers

HarperCollins books may be purchased for educational, business, or sales promotional use. For information, please email the Special Markets Department at SPsales@harpercollins.com.

FIRST EDITION

DESIGNED BY LEAH CARLSON-STANISIC

Photographs and styling by Melina Hammer
Personal photographs from Julia's archive
Photographs on pages iv, vi, xviii, xxx, 27, 118, 148, 238, 258, 254 by Winifred Au

Library of Congress Cataloging-in-Publication Data has been applied for.

ISBN 978-0-06-299333-5

21 22 23 24 25 TC 10 9 8 7 6 5 4 3 2 1

IN MEMORY OF GEORGINE + TURK

———

Georgine taught us that you're never too old to give back,
make a friend, or change your mind about something.

Turk was the greatest cat that ever lived, our sweet boy.

CONTENTS

INTRODUCTION

I LOVED MAKING THIS BOOK. It's all about healthy comfort food and it explores and celebrates the many definitions of "healthy" and "comfort."

It's not only the most personal book I've ever written, it's also the most practical. It has ten useful chapters including weeknight go-tos and vegan one-pot meals that are great whether or not you're vegan. There's a chapter that's all salad dressings and easy sauces. There are Seven Lists at the back of the book that cover everything from what to do with leftover buttermilk to prompts for meaningful mealtime conversations. There are also reference lists of all of the vegetarian recipes (87!), vegan ones (42!), additional dairy/egg-free recipes (21!), and gluten-free ones (a whopping 106!). There's a chapter of just chicken recipes. There's something for everyone and all of it is simple.

Since I'm a home cook just like you, when I write recipes, I think about the entire experience of making the recipe, from shopping to cleaning up. Home cooking is, after all, so much more than cooking. It's planning and schlepping and remembering what needs to be used up and wiping down surfaces and peeling things and washing dishes. In my recipes, if you can use one bowl instead of two, I'll never tell you to use the extra bowl. I won't tell you how long to cook something without also telling you what should happen within that time. Our kitchens are all different. My stove may not be as hot as yours, so what takes me eight minutes might take you five. I get that.

All of these recipes also use widely available, affordable ingredients. If I can't find it within half an hour of my house (which is in a rural area), you won't find it in this book. And I will forever champion the belief that no one is required to spend a lot of money, time, or effort to make a good dinner. Delicious food does not have to be complicated. Cooking, when it's at its best, is a way to take care of each other, not compete with each other. Remember that for every beautiful food photo you see on Instagram (or in this book for that matter), there's a tall pile of dishes in a sink somewhere. Literally and figuratively.

I TALK TO OTHER HOME COOKS ALL OF THE TIME.

Whether it's my father, my mother-in-law, my closest friends, or the many people I've gotten to know online and in person on book tours, I am always asking people what they're cooking and also what keeps them from cooking. So many of us love to cook, but we don't always have the time we wish we had in the kitchen. We want to support our local vendors but don't always have room in our schedules to shop at different stores. We care about where our food comes from, even if we don't always make it to the farmers' market. I get it. I love to cook. I have dedicated my life to it. I work from home. My kitchen is basically my office. But sometimes even I don't feel like cooking.

As much as I believe in cooking at home and the thought of our collective power as home cooks can make me emotional, sometimes I just don't feel like peeling an onion. I will almost always choose a nonstick skillet over a stainless steel one because it's just so easy to clean. This is also why I love to grill (see the love letter I wrote to my gas grill on page 64). I'd much rather quickly scrape the hot grates than soak and scrub a pot. What I've come to realize is that you can believe in home cooking and also sometimes feel tired of it. That's okay! Both of these things can be true at the same time. This cookbook celebrates the marathon, not the sprint. It's for everyday home cooks who sometimes just need a recipe that doesn't require chopping (see Llubav's Green Spaghetti on page 3, Ricotta + Potato Chip Fish Cakes with Peas on page 17, and Green Chile Braised Chicken Thighs with Pinto Beans on page 85).

The recipes in this book aren't just easy, they're comforting. If you're looking for trendy, I'm not your girl. Nostalgia, though a complicated thing, informs so many of my recipes. The food I most love, and especially love to share in my cookbooks, stems from my memories. It's inspired by so much of the stuff that I grew up with and so much of the stuff that glues the various members of my family, both biological and chosen, together. My recipes are for and about the communities I'm most connected to. Some are from my grandmother, others from my mother-in-law, many are from dishes I've cooked for my friends; others are inspired by people I've met through work, and many come directly from the meals my wife and I cook in our weekly volunteer shift at an organization called Angel Food East. All of these are cozy meals. Meals that don't try to wow you, but hug you.

I describe every single recipe in this book as healthy and encourage a personal definition of the word. After all, what does "healthy" even mean? How do you define it? I believe it has a wide, generous definition that's all about freedom. To me, it's as much about what I'm eating as it is how I feel when I'm eating. It's my entire relationship to food and, like any other relationship, the healthiest one I can aim for involves tons of respect, patience, and love.

At its best, committing to eating in a healthy way also allows me to broaden my lens outside of myself. Healthy food isn't just what I eat. It's also about connecting myself more closely with where my food comes from and honoring, compensating, and protecting the people who grow, harvest, distribute, clean, stock, and sell the food I eat. It's connecting myself to the person sitting next to me at my kitchen table, and also strengthening the connections I have to the people in my neighborhood. Healthy food connects the dots. It invites gratitude. Healthy food, in my book (like literally, this book), does not have any room for guilt. It's full of agency to pick and choose. It comes from a place of love, not fear. It's about feeling full, in a truly holistic sense, and has zero to do with deprivation of any kind.

When it comes to the food itself, what we're actually cooking, "healthy" means something different for each of us. If there were one way to eat that worked for everyone's bodies that felt easy and fun, we would have a whole lot less to talk about (and many companies would no longer benefit financially from us feeling bad about ourselves and our bodies). From a logistic standpoint, all the recipes in this book are inspired by the low-carb-high-quality life that my wife, Grace—who lives with type 1 diabetes—and I share at home, plus the meals we cook for our community in our volunteer work, which asks us to consider the medical needs of our homebound clients. This means that all of my recipes have a light hand with ingredients like butter and sour cream (but are not afraid of them!), are mindful of excessive sugar, and favor plants and grains. Most important, every single recipe is easygoing. Taking care of yourself and the people around you should help alleviate stress, not pile it on.

What I have learned from bringing my previous books into the world is that sharing useful information with fellow home cooks is one of my favorite things to do. It makes me feel like we're a big team.

Not only can we can cook, we can invite someone over because there's something on the stove anyway and it's no big deal. We can use food to gather large groups of people in meaningful ways. We can make celebrations sweeter with our baking, we can mark accomplishments with festive meals, and we can offer tangible comfort in times of grief and crisis. We can support our neighbors, whether it's by being intentional about where we shop for our ingredients or making a double batch of a recipe to share with someone. We can remember that the resourcefulness and flexibility we exercise in our kitchens can be extended outside of them.

I WAS REMINDED OF ALL OF THIS WHILE MAKING THIS BOOK.

I turned in the very first draft of my manuscript at the end of February 2020, just weeks before New York State, where I live, went into lockdown to prevent COVID-19 from taking even more lives in its devastating grip. I photographed it with Melina Hammer, a gifted photographer who also happens to live ten minutes away from me, during April 2020. We did this while witnessing the pandemic ravage so many communities, most especially marginalized communities already fighting chronic, systemic racism and injustice.

These circumstances continue to remind me that no matter what's happening in the world, the people who take care of other people are always essential. Not only are they essential, they're everyday heroes, whether they administer care, stock grocery shelves, clean schools, make sure everyone is fed, or advocate for all of our rights. I am reminded that we can, if we haven't already, figure out how we can be everyday heroes in our own communities.

While I care deeply about giving you trustworthy recipes, pretty photos to show you what they look like, and stories to tell you what they all mean to me, what I care most about is who you're cooking for, including you. The tools I'm so happy and grateful to share aren't just for getting a meal prepared, they're also for being helpful, involved, caring citizens. Home cooks are helpers. The rest of this book contains easy recipes, yes, but it also contains page after page of ways to take, and offer, care.

Like all books, cookbooks are relics of the time they were made. Making this one right now was a profound experience. It has cemented for me that daily home cooking is a practice. Within its repetition, it reveals that the most important things in life are both simple and relentless. We must keep at it. And what a gift it is to do so.

MY WIFE GRACE, OUR DOGS
(HOPE & WINKY) + ME, 2020

FIVE LISTS

Each of these Five Lists includes five items that make my kitchen an easy, comfortable place for me to cook. Most cookbooks include a few pages dedicated to all the things that make a kitchen a kitchen. Chances are if you own just one cookbook besides this one, you probably have access to a substantial pantry and equipment section somewhere. I've even written sections like these in the past. And the truth is, I find them stressful. To write and to read. Like what if something I swear by isn't helpful to you? What if I leave out a kitchen tool you swear by? If I don't have an entire knife set, am I an imposter? (No, by the way, I'm not, and neither are you.) Use the stuff that works for you, that you can afford, that you borrow from a family member or a friend, and whatever else makes your kitchen work for you. In the spirit of my Seven Lists (see page 229), here are twenty-five things that make my kitchen work for me. These are not meant to be exhaustive lists, but if they offer you something that makes your cooking life more comfortable, I'll consider it a victory.

FIVE THINGS THAT ARE ALWAYS IN MY REFRIGERATOR

EGGS: My anxiety meter rises when we're low on eggs, so I always buy at least two dozen at a time. Note that every recipe in this book that includes eggs was tested with large eggs.

CORN TORTILLAS: You know what's great in a taco? Just about anything. That's why we always have corn tortillas in our fridge. The best way I know to warm corn tortillas is to heat them directly over the flame of your gas stove, using tongs to flip them. Once they're a little bit charred, wrap them in a kitchen towel, and let them sit and steam amongst themselves for a minute before serving. No gas stove? No problem. Do the same in a hot cast-iron skillet.

DIJON MUSTARD: My next book might have to be an all-mustard book. I just love it. It wakes things up, thickens dressings, and generally adds spark.

KIMCHI: Ever since I worked on *The Kimchi Chronicles*, a PBS cooking show and companion cookbook, I've been a regular kimchi consumer. When I'm not having a bite straight from the jar, I'm putting it on a bowl of rice and topping it with a fried egg, making kimchi fried rice, or topping avocado toast with it. I also love to chop it finely and mix it into tuna or chicken salad (page 243). And don't pour the liquid from the jar down the drain! It's so valuable. Whisk it together with equal parts mayonnaise to make the easiest, best salad dressing.

BETTER THAN BOUILLON: In my dreams I'm a home cook who always has a container of homemade stock in the fridge made from the peels and ends and bones of whatever I last cooked. Yes, I do this sometimes, but not all the time. And for those times when I don't, there's Better Than Bouillon, which I whisk into boiling water for instant stock that might not be *the real deal* but is close enough when you need a little something more than water. I keep the Vegetarian No Chicken Base on hand since I can use it anywhere I would use either chicken or vegetable stock. This is what I'm referring to any time I mention bouillon paste dissolved in boiling water as an alternative to stock (you can also use your preferred brand of bouillon cubes).

FIVE THINGS THAT ARE ALWAYS IN MY SPICE DRAWER

SALT: My counter is naked without a bowl of Diamond Crystal kosher salt on it. I use it for everything, whether seasoning vegetables before roasting them, adding it to boiling water before cooking pasta, and even for cleaning my wooden cutting boards (sprinkle it on, use a halved lemon like a sponge, and there you go). I also keep a little teacup full of Maldon salt for sprinkling on finished dishes like roasted potatoes, boiled eggs, and salads. I could live without Maldon if I *had* to, but I'd have a very hard time being without kosher salt.

OLD BAY: No, I'm not a Baltimore native, but I do love Old Bay Seasoning as if it were my hometown (it originated there, and Baltimoreans have a lot of warranted pride about it). A combination of celery salt, red and black pepper, and paprika, it's the mix of spices I most love already packaged in a perfect little tin. I call for it in so many places because it's a lot easier to reach for it than all those spices by themselves. Try it on your popcorn!

GROUND GINGER: I try to bake without using a ton of sugar because I like things that are barely sweet, plus it makes it easier for Grace to enjoy stuff since less sugar means having to take less insulin. I find the less sugar I use, the more flavor I need to add to compensate. Enter ground ginger, which makes so many baked goods taste full of warm spice without adding any sweetener.

PIMENTÓN (SMOKED SPANISH PAPRIKA): Made of smoked and ground peppers, pimentón makes everything it touches taste like it's been cooked for a long time over an open fire. I love it in stews and chilis and especially love it when I'm making vegetarian or vegan dishes since it adds an almost meaty smokiness to things without any actual meat or smoke. It comes in hot and sweet varieties—feel free to use whichever you prefer depending on your preferences (I tested every recipe it appears in with sweet pimentón because it's what I keep on hand).

GARLIC POWDER: I don't think of garlic powder as a substitute for fresh garlic, but rather its own separate thing. You know how a slice of pizza tastes extra savory when you sprinkle garlic powder on top? I like to bring that effect to so many other things, whether it's shaking it on chicken before grilling it or adding it to homemade ranch dressing.

FIVE TOOLS I SWEAR BY

HANDHELD ELECTRIC MIXER: My grandparents gave me a KitchenAid stand mixer for my bat mitzvah (so sweet) and, more than twenty years later, it's still going strong. That's likely because I rarely feel like pulling it out. I use it when I do things for a special occasion, like when I made my cousin's wedding cake, but in general I don't think my irregular use warrants real estate on my kitchen counter. Enter the handheld electric mixer, which can do lots of heavy lifting without actually being heavy to lift. Plus you just pop off the beaters and throw them in the dishwasher and it's no big deal. It's what I use when I want to make homemade whipped cream but don't feel like whisking it by hand, or when I want to whip egg whites for Beatrice's Bubaleh (page 167) with ease.

SWING-A-WAY JAR OPENER: Speaking of my grandparents, my grandmother introduced this tool to me when I was a kid and I really can't imagine life without it. A slim device, it grips the lids of jars and bottle caps with ease and gives you enough leverage to open anything, which is especially great if you have arthritis or any similar condition.

A VERY SMALL WHISK: I never used a small whisk until Grace brought one into our kitchen. At first I just thought "clutter!" but I've come to love it. When you just want to mix a little something together, like spiking some mayonnaise with lime juice and salt, it's perfect. And it's adorable and makes me happy and that's worth something.

TOASTER OVEN: I use ours all the time, whether it's to make a piece of toast, to warm up leftover roasted potatoes or carrots, to cook a few frozen fish fingers, or to bake a couple of cookies from my stash of frozen cookie dough. Since I use it every single day, I think it's more than worthy of a spot on the kitchen counter.

DIGITAL SCALE: The world can be divided into two types of people: those who use measuring cups for baking, and those who use a digital scale (actually, three types if you include those who don't bake at all). I am on Team Digital Scale. Not only do they keep everything accurate, they also mean you don't have to clean up a bunch of different cups and spoons each time you bake. You just weigh out one ingredient in your mixing bowl, set the scale back to zero, and add the next. Note that all of the recipes include both weight measurements and cup-and-spoon measurements, so no matter which way you measure, I've got you covered.

FIVE THINGS THAT ARE ALWAYS IN MY CUPBOARD

OLIVE OIL: One of the things I truly can't cook without, I use olive oil every single day and in almost everything I make. My preferred brand is California Olive Ranch. I also use olive oil cooking spray a lot, whether to coat the surface of a nonstick skillet before cooking eggs, spraying a cake pan before the batter goes in, or for spraying Almond Chicken Cutlets for Grace (page 77) before baking. You can buy a can or, better yet, get an oil sprayer (Misto makes a good one) and refill it yourself.

VINEGARS: A collection of vinegars in your cupboard means that you can easily take salad dressings, pickles, sauces, and more into so many different directions. The three I use the most are apple cider vinegar (I even sometimes just splash a little into seltzer for a kombucha-like spritzer), red wine vinegar, and unseasoned rice vinegar.

TAHINI: A paste made of ground sesame seeds, tahini is an ambrosial ingredient that makes things taste and feel rich and creamy without adding any dairy. My preferred brand is Soom. Always stir your tahini well before measuring.

BEANS: If there's a can of beans or a bag of dried beans in my cupboard, I know there's a meal waiting. They're so versatile, affordable, more environmentally friendly than animal protein, and just downright delicious. I am a bean lover and while I don't have a big brand preference when it comes to canned beans, I swear by Rancho Gordo for dried beans (ranchogordo.com for all your bean needs). Any recipe that calls for a can of beans can be substituted with an equal weight of beans you've cooked.

WHOLE WHEAT FLOUR: I bake primarily with whole wheat flour (I'm a King Arthur girl) because I like its nutty flavor, it feels wholesome, and it has more fiber than all-purpose flour. Feel free to substitute all-purpose flour or your favorite all-purpose gluten-free flour.

FIVE THINGS I COUNT ON FOR GOOD KITCHEN VIBES

MUSIC: I can't think of anything that transforms a kitchen more quickly, easily, or effectively than music. Turn it on, turn it up.

CLOTH NAPKINS: I rarely use a tablecloth, almost always forget about candles, and polish my silverware once a year if I'm lucky. But I try to always use cloth napkins when we sit down to eat. They just make everything feel adult.

OLD DISHES: Although I never got to meet my maternal grandmother, I have her collection of china and use the dishes regularly. Grace and I also have lots of other plates and bowls passed down from family members or made by ceramicist friends. It feels so different to eat a meal off a dish that has some history. And if one slips in the sink and breaks or chips, at least it's because we're using them and not letting them collect dust in a cupboard. Life is short—use your nice dishes every day.

SILVERWARE: My paternal grandmother gave me her silverware a number of years ago and we now use it daily. I am too lazy to keep it polished and shiny, but who cares. It makes everything, even a bowl of cereal or stirring half-and-half into coffee, feel a little special. We also sometimes pick up spoons and forks at antique stores and just add them to the drawer. I feel strongly that it doesn't matter if your silverware doesn't match.

CONTAINERS: Having a lot of containers—with matching lids!—makes me feel secure. I like using pint- and quart-sized deli containers and glass containers with lids that snap on because you can see what's inside of them and they stack well.

SIMPLY JULIA

1

ELEVEN WEEKNIGHT GO-TOS

LLUBAV'S GREEN SPAGHETTI

One of the nicest things that happened when I first met Grace was meeting her friends, including Llubav, a gifted artist and a mother of two. This green spaghetti, inspired by her cousin Shuggie, is one of Llubav's go-tos. It's a winner and is great for weeknight cooking since you don't have to chop a thing! You just blend some spinach, torn kale, fresh basil, and garlic with feta, cream cheese, and olive oil to make a fresh but also rich sauce that wraps itself around spaghetti. I use whole wheat spaghetti here not only because it's got a bit more nutritional bang for its buck, but also because its nuttiness really goes so well with the sauce. The sauce would also be good stirred into rice or crushed boiled potatoes. You could add a package of frozen peas or broccoli to the pasta pot at the end of cooking for another dose of vegetables (without any chopping). You could also top each portion with a fried egg for a boost of protein. Thank you, Llubav, for sharing it.

Serves 4

Kosher salt

1 pound [453 g] whole wheat spaghetti (or whatever type of pasta you'd like)

5 ounces [141 g] fresh baby spinach

6 large leaves fresh kale (any type), tough stems discarded, torn into large pieces

1 large handful fresh basil leaves (about 12 large leaves)

2 garlic cloves, peeled

½ cup [50 g] crumbled feta cheese, plus extra for serving

3 tablespoons cream cheese

3 tablespoons extra-virgin olive oil

Set a large pot of water to boil and salt it generously. Add the spaghetti to the pot and cook according to the package directions.

Meanwhile, place the spinach, kale, basil, garlic, feta cheese, cream cheese, and olive oil in a blender and add 1 cup [240 ml] of the boiling salted water from the pasta pot. Puree until smooth and season to taste with salt (it might need quite a bit depending on how salty your water is—don't be shy!).

Drain the spaghetti in a colander and then return it to the now-empty pot. Add the green sauce and stir well to combine.

Serve immediately with extra crumbled feta cheese on top.

SESAME RICE BOWLS WITH
TOFU, QUICKLES + PEANUT SAUCE

SESAME RICE BOWLS WITH TOFU, QUICKLES + PEANUT SAUCE

This is just the sort of thing I make all the time for dinner since it happens quickly and rarely requires a trip to the store (it's full of ingredients we always have on hand). Friends of mine who have kids also tell me this is great for them because everyone can customize their own bowls (plus peanut sauce usually helps the vegetables go down). Making this recipe requires a bit of multitasking, but the multitasking happens in harmony and gives you a sense of confidence in the kitchen. Cooking a meal often means making a few simple parts that come together to make a satisfying whole. This is not just how I like to cook, it's also how I most like to eat.

Serves 4

For the tofu

One 14-ounce [397 g] container extra-firm tofu, drained

¼ cup [60 ml] canola oil (or other neutral oil such as vegetable)

2 teaspoons soy sauce

2 teaspoons fish sauce (skip or substitute extra soy sauce if you're vegetarian or vegan)

1 to 3 teaspoons chili garlic sauce (such as sambal; add to taste or feel free to leave out)

For the rice

1 tablespoon canola oil (or other neutral oil such as vegetable)

1 tablespoon toasted sesame oil

1 tablespoon sesame seeds

1 cup [200 g] long-grain white rice

1½ cups [360 ml] water

1 teaspoon kosher salt

For the quickles

¼ cup [60 ml] rice vinegar

2 tablespoons water

1 tablespoon granulated sugar

1 teaspoon kosher salt

1 English cucumber, ends discarded, thinly sliced

2 large carrots, peeled and thinly sliced on the diagonal

For the peanut sauce

¼ cup [63 g] creamy peanut butter (unsweetened or sweetened, use whatever you have)

¼ cup [60 ml] boiling water

2 tablespoons rice vinegar

1 teaspoon soy sauce

¼ teaspoon kosher salt

First, press the tofu
Wrap the tofu in a clean kitchen towel. Put a cutting board on top of the tofu and then put something heavy on top of it, like a Dutch oven, and let it sit for at least 15 minutes and up to an hour (this is a good time to get all your other ingredients ready). Pressing helps to remove excess moisture.

Next, make the rice
Place the tablespoon each of canola and sesame oils in a medium saucepan over medium heat. Add the sesame seeds and rice and cook, stirring, until the rice begins to brown and smell nutty, about 2 minutes. Add the water and salt. Bring the mixture to a boil, turn the heat to low, cover the pot, and simmer until the liquid is absorbed and the rice is tender, about 15 minutes. Turn off the heat, uncover the pot, and place a clean kitchen towel in between the rice and the lid. Cover the pot and let the rice sit off the heat, with its towel to absorb extra steam, for 10 minutes before fluffing with a spoon.

While the rice cooks, make the quickles
Place the rice vinegar, water, sugar, and salt in a medium bowl and whisk until the sugar and salt

dissolve. Add the cucumber and carrots and stir well to combine. Let the vegetables sit while you prepare the tofu and everything else. Give the vegetables a stir every so often.

Next, finish the tofu
Place the canola oil in a large nonstick skillet over medium-high heat. Crumble in the pressed tofu so it's roughly the size of beans and cook it, without stirring!, until it's a little browned and crisp on the bottom, about 7 minutes. Drizzle the soy sauce, fish sauce, and chili garlic sauce on the tofu and continue to cook it, this time stirring, until it's very fragrant and quite dry and crisp, about 5 more minutes. Start with just 1 teaspoon of the chili garlic sauce and increase the amount to your taste

(or leave it out if you're cooking for little kids or anyone else who might not like any heat . . . I like all the heat!).

Last, make the peanut sauce
Place the peanut butter, boiling water, rice vinegar, soy sauce, and salt in a small bowl and whisk well to combine. Reserve the sauce.

To serve
Divide the rice and tofu among 4 bowls. Drain the quickles and divide them among the bowls (discard the excess brine or save to quickly pickle some more vegetables). Drizzle with the peanut sauce and serve immediately.

DOUG'S TEX-MEX TURKEY MEATBALLS

When I was growing up, my dad used to regularly make what we lovingly referred to as Doug's Famous Tex-Mex Meatloaf on the weekends. He swapped in crushed tortilla chips for the standard breadcrumbs and salsa for the eggs and seasoning. He also loaded it with cheddar cheese. Simple to make and irresistible to eat, it was something my entire family looked forward to. I like making the mixture into roasted meatballs rather than meatloaf because they cook a lot faster (I'm impatient) and they're easier to serve (no crumbly slices). You can also bake these, freeze them, and then reheat them in a 300°F [150°C] oven until warmed through. Serve with rice and beans, roasted sweet potato wedges and broccoli, mashed cauliflower, green beans . . . whatever!

Makes 20 meatballs (serves 4 with a side dish, or 2 with just a salad)

For the meatballs

3 cups [150 g] corn tortilla chips (with salt! not unsalted! but if they're unsalted, just add an extra ½ teaspoon salt to the meatballs)

1 pound [453 g] ground turkey (preferably dark meat, but white meat works, too)

1 cup [250 g] jarred tomato salsa (whatever brand and level of spice you like)

1 teaspoon kosher salt

1 cup [110 g] coarsely grated sharp cheddar cheese

For the sauce

½ cup [125 g] jarred tomato salsa

1 cup [227 g] sour cream

First, make the meatballs
Preheat your oven to 425°F [220°C]. Line a sheet pan with parchment paper and set it aside.

Place the tortilla chips in a large plastic bag and seal the bag. Crush the chips with a rolling pin or a wine bottle until the crumbs are very fine and then transfer them to a large bowl. Add the ground turkey, salsa, salt, and cheese. Use your hands to mix everything together.

Form the mixture into 20 equal-sized meatballs. It's helpful to divide the mixture in half and then in half again and so on to make sure the meatballs are the same size. Wetting your hands with cold water will help keep the mixture from sticking to them.

You can also make the meatballs a little smaller or a little larger—just keep them all about the same size so that they cook evenly.

Evenly space the meatballs on the prepared sheet pan and roast until they're firm to the touch and cooked through (break into one to check it), about 20 minutes.

Next, make the sauce
Place the salsa and sour cream in a small bowl and stir well to combine.

And serve
Serve the meatballs warm with the sauce on the side for dipping.

MY DAD + ME, 1996

SWEDISH TURKEY MEATBALLS

Having lived in many apartments in New York City in my adult life and having helped many friends and family members settle into their homes, I'm pretty familiar with Ikea. The best way to get through the store, like all of us who have done many an Ikea run know, is to first eat a serving of their Swedish meatballs and then tackle your shopping list since all things stressful are made easier with a full stomach. These turkey meatballs are my version of their famous meatballs. They're so easy to make and are great served over egg noodles, rice, mashed potatoes, or thick slices of toasted pumpernickel bread (anything to soak up the sauce). A little cranberry sauce, lingonberry jam, or Cherry + Allspice Sauce (page 153) is delicious here, too. If it's easier for you, you can bake the meatballs as instructed for Doug's Tex-Mex Turkey Meatballs (page 8), and then heat them up in the sauce just before serving. They're not quite as tender this way, but they're still very good.

Makes 20 meatballs (serves 4 with rice or noodles and a vegetable, or 2 with just a salad or a vegetable)

1 pound [453 g] ground turkey (preferably dark meat, but white meat works, too)

1 large egg, lightly beaten

½ cup [35 g] dried breadcrumbs (preferably panko)

½ teaspoon ground allspice

¼ teaspoon freshly ground nutmeg

1½ teaspoons kosher salt

1½ teaspoons freshly ground black pepper

1 cup [240 ml] chicken stock (homemade, store-bought, or bouillon paste dissolved in boiling water)

1 cup [227 g] sour cream, preferably at room temperature

1 tablespoon Worcestershire sauce

1 large handful fresh Italian parsley, finely chopped (optional, but if you use it, a little stem is fine)

Place the turkey, egg, breadcrumbs, allspice, nutmeg, salt, and pepper in a large bowl and mix together well with your hands.

Form the mixture into 20 equal-sized meatballs. It's helpful to divide the mixture in half and then in half again and so on to make sure the meatballs are the same size. Wetting your hands with cold water will help keep the mixture from sticking to them. You can also make the meatballs a little smaller or a little larger—just keep them all about the same size so that they cook evenly.

Place the stock, sour cream, and Worcestershire sauce in a medium bowl and whisk well to combine.

Transfer the mixture to a large nonstick skillet over high heat (if you have a non-metal whisk, you can just whisk the mixture in the skillet). The second the mixture comes to a boil, turn the heat to low and add the meatballs in an even layer.

Simmer the meatballs uncovered, using tongs to turn them every so often to make sure they cook evenly, until the meatballs are very firm to the touch and cooked through (break into one to check it), about 20 minutes.

Sprinkle the meatballs with the parsley (if using). Serve hot, making sure everyone gets plenty of sauce with their serving.

SIZZLE BURGERS

At the end of each episode of my podcast, *Keep Calm and Cook On*, I ask my guest what their favorite thing to eat was when they were growing up. I love this question because everyone kind of melts when I ask it and they always have a good story (see page 234 for more questions like this one). Once I asked my mother-in-law, Elaine, what types of things she cooked for Grace when she was growing up. When she mentioned "sizzle burgers," Grace's eyes got really wide. "I forgot about sizzle burgers!" she said. And I knew immediately that I had to know all about them. Elaine said she started making these burgers when she and Chris, my father-in-law, were first married, and that he still loves them. She browns the burgers in a skillet, takes them out to rest, and then adds onions and butter to the skillet and lets them get all melty. At the end, she adds a splash of Worcestershire and a little water to make the onions even saucier. She serves the patties and onions over rice, which I highly recommend. You can also serve them with egg noodles, on a bun (don't forget napkins), or with mashed potatoes. They're also great with simple sautéed or roasted vegetables. When I first made them for Grace, she said the kitchen smelled like her childhood. I can't think of a better compliment.

Serves 4

1 pound [453 g] ground turkey (preferably dark meat, but white meat works, too, or you can use beef)

Kosher salt

Freshly ground black pepper

2 tablespoons extra-virgin olive oil

1 large Vidalia or yellow onion, thinly sliced

2 tablespoons unsalted butter

¼ cup [60 ml] water

2 tablespoons Worcestershire sauce

Divide the turkey into 4 equal portions and shape each into a patty about 4 inches [10 cm] across. Season the patties generously with salt and pepper on both sides.

Place the oil in a large, heavy skillet (preferably cast-iron) over high heat. Once the oil shimmers and the pan is very hot, place the burgers in the pan. Cook until a crust forms and the bottoms of each burger are dark brown and don't give you a hard time when you flip them with a spatula, about 5 minutes. Turn each burger and cook until the other side is also browned and the burgers are firm to the touch, about another 5 minutes.

Transfer the burgers to a serving dish and tent with aluminum foil to keep them warm.

Place the onions and butter in the skillet and turn the heat to medium. Cook, stirring now and then, until the onions are just tender and browned in spots, about 10 minutes. Add the water and Worcestershire sauce to the skillet and cook, scraping the bottom of the skillet with a wooden spoon to release any flavorful bits, until the mixture is boiling, about 1 minute. Top the burgers with the onions and pan juices and serve immediately.

PORK TENDERLOIN PICCATA

One night, Grace and I were both really hungry and ready for dinner and I was going to throw a pork tender-loin in the oven to roast, which is a very easy and logical thing to do and honestly doesn't take that long. But the idea of waiting for the oven to heat and the pork to cook and then rest just felt like an eternity. So I cut the pork into thin slices, seasoned them, and browned them in a skillet. I threw some capers, wine, and lemon juice in the skillet and finished the whole thing with a little butter, à la piccata, and we had the most delicious dinner in no time. This recipe has become a regular for us, and it goes well with lots of things, whether a simple salad or some garlicky broccoli rabe with white beans, or mashed potatoes, or lemony spaghetti . . . you get the idea.

Serves 4

1 cup [125 g] all-purpose flour

1 teaspoon kosher salt, plus more for serving

1 teaspoon freshly ground black pepper

1½ pounds [680 g] pork tenderloin, cut into ¼-inch- [½-cm-] thick slices

3 tablespoons extra-virgin olive oil, plus more if needed

1 tablespoon unsalted butter, plus 2 extra tablespoons cut into small pieces for the sauce

3 tablespoons drained capers

½ cup [120 ml] dry white wine (or chicken stock)

3 tablespoons fresh lemon juice

Place the flour, salt, and pepper in a shallow bowl and whisk well to combine. Coat the pork slices on both sides with the flour, knocking off any excess (you just want a light coating). Discard any flour that remains.

Place the olive oil and the tablespoon of butter in a large nonstick skillet over medium-high heat. Once the butter melts and begins to bubble, add as many pieces of pork to the pan as can fit while still leaving a little space between them. Cook, flipping once, until deeply browned on both sides and cooked through, about 2 minutes per side. Transfer the cooked pork to a serving platter while you continue to cook the rest (add a little oil to the pan in between batches if needed).

Once all your pork is cooked through, add the capers to whatever fat remains in the skillet. Once they start to sizzle, add the white wine and bring to a boil. Let the mixture boil for a minute just to reduce a little bit and to cook off the raw alcohol taste. Turn the heat to low, add the lemon juice and final 2 tablespoons of butter, and stir with a wooden spoon to loosen up any bits stuck to the bottom and to make a smooth, emulsified sauce (if it doesn't emulsify, don't worry, it will still taste wonderful). Pour the sauce evenly over the pork. Serve immediately.

SAEV-KIMCHI-JJIGAE (SHRIMP + KIMCHI STEW)

About a decade ago I worked on *The Kimchi Chronicles*, a PBS show, and its companion cookbook. I got to travel all around South Korea for a month and even had the chance to visit Jeju Island, the province south of the Korean Peninsula. The biggest highlight was getting to meet the haenyeos, the celebrated female divers in Jeju who harvest seafood and seaweed (which they've been doing for hundreds of years). Getting to meet some of them, standing on the beach as they donned their black wetsuits and gigantic goggles, left a lasting impression. I can't eat any type of seafood without picturing them.

I ate more bowls of kimchi-jjigae (kimchi stew) in Korea than I can count. It tastes like it took a long time to cook, but it's truly one of the quickest, most satisfying dishes I know since all the work is really in the making of the kimchi, which you can do if you'd like (fermentation is fun!) or you can just buy a jar.

I've seen and tasted kimchi-jjigae made so many different ways, at its simplest just kimchi and water simmered together, but often with an anchovy or seaweed stock at the base. Many versions have pork, some tuna. This version, made with some onions cooked in sesame oil, plus garlic, kimchi, water, and shrimp, is my favorite. Feel free to substitute clams, or cubes of your favorite fish or tofu, instead of the shrimp. Serve with rice.

Serves 4

One 16-ounce [453 g] jar cabbage kimchi (including its juice!)

2 tablespoons canola oil (or any other neutral oil such as vegetable)

1 tablespoon toasted sesame oil

1 large white or yellow onion, sliced into thin half-moons (or 1 bunch scallions, thinly sliced)

6 garlic cloves, minced

1 pound [453 g] shrimp, peeled and deveined

1 tablespoon soy sauce

Kosher salt

Hot cooked rice, for serving

Open the jar of kimchi and use a pair of scissors to roughly chop the kimchi directly in its container (I learned this tip from a few Korean home cooks and it saves you washing a board and a knife). Don't worry about cutting the kimchi too evenly, you just want to avoid having any huge pieces that are hard to eat off of your spoon later. Put the jar to the side (you'll use it all in a moment).

Warm the oils in a medium saucepan over medium-high heat. Add the onion and cook, stirring now and then, until just beginning to soften, about 5 minutes. Add the garlic and cook until just

fragrant, about 30 seconds. Add the kimchi and its juice. Fill the now-empty kimchi jar with water and swish it around to loosen any stuck bits of flavor and then pour the water into the saucepan. Turn the heat to high and bring the mixture to a boil. Turn the heat to low so that the mixture relaxes to a simmer, add the shrimp, cover the pot, and cook just until the shrimp are firm and opaque, about 4 minutes. Stir in the soy sauce and season the stew to taste with salt as needed (it might not need any or it might need a few pinches—it depends on how salty the kimchi is and your preferences . . . trust yourself here). Serve immediately over hot rice.

FANCY WEEKNIGHT SALMON SALAD

Want something that feels impressive but is also super simple to prepare? Enter this salmon (which could easily be any type of fish) that you roast quickly with some mushrooms and then toss everything with arugula, avocado for creaminess, roasted almonds for crunch and salt, a simple dressing, and pickled shallots that you make while the fish roasts. Feel free to double the amount of pickled shallots and keep extra in a jar in the refrigerator. Use them to top salads, tacos, and sandwiches.

Serves 4

1½ pounds [680 g] salmon, in one large piece, skin and bones discarded (doesn't matter how thick the piece is)

1 pound [453 g] assorted mushrooms, tough stems discarded, roughly chopped

Cooking spray (my preference is olive oil spray, but use whatever you have)

Kosher salt

½ teaspoon freshly ground black pepper

1 large or 2 medium shallots, thinly sliced (about a large handful sliced shallots, or red onion)

½ teaspoon granulated sugar

2 tablespoons red wine vinegar

2 tablespoons extra-virgin olive oil

2 tablespoons soy sauce

2 tablespoons fresh lemon juice (or just more red wine vinegar)

2 tablespoons well-stirred tahini

5 ounces [141 g] fresh baby arugula

2 ripe avocados, peeled, pitted, and diced

¼ cup [35 g] roasted, salted almonds, roughly chopped

Preheat your oven to 425°F [220°C].

Line a sheet pan with parchment paper. Place the salmon in the middle of the pan and surround it with the mushrooms. Coat the fish and mushrooms generously with cooking spray and sprinkle everything with ½ teaspoon salt and the pepper. Roast until the fish flakes easily and is opaque in the center (test by poking it with a paring knife), and the mushrooms are tender and browned in spots, about 25 minutes.

Meanwhile, place ½ teaspoon salt in a small bowl with the shallots, sugar, and red wine vinegar.

Stir well to dissolve the salt and sugar and let the mixture sit while the fish roasts.

Place the olive oil, soy sauce, lemon juice, and tahini in a large bowl and whisk until smooth. Season the dressing to taste with salt. Add the arugula to the bowl and toss well to combine. Transfer the arugula to a large serving platter.

Break the fish into large pieces and place them on top of the arugula. Top the fish with the roasted mushrooms and top those with the shallots and their pickling liquid. Top with the avocado and almonds. Serve immediately.

RICOTTA + POTATO CHIP FISH CAKES WITH PEAS

An homage to the salmon patties I got to enjoy one morning at Narobia's Grits & Gravy in Savannah, Georgia (which I learned about thanks to Mashama Bailey's amazing episode of *Chef's Table*), these fish cakes rely on canned salmon, one of the most convenient and reliable things to keep in your cupboard.

Since the salmon is already cooked and void of bones and skin, it's just a matter of mixing it with a few other ingredients, forming it into patties, and giving them a nice crust in a hot skillet. Instead of the typical eggs and breadcrumbs, I use a mixture of ricotta cheese, which gives you a sort of lox and cream cheese effect, and crushed potato chips, which give you a sort of fish-and-chips effect (plus they keep these gluten-free if that's important to you). After you brown the fish cakes, you add some frozen peas and half-and-half to the skillet, which makes a bright green bed for the fish cakes. You could also skip the peas and serve the fish cakes on toasted potato buns slicked with mayonnaise and piled with shredded lettuce and sliced pickles.

Serves 4

One 2-ounce [56 g] bag potato chips (preferably sour cream and onion–flavored)

Two 6-ounce [170 g] cans wild pink salmon packed in water, well-drained

1 cup [235 g] whole milk ricotta cheese

1 tablespoon Old Bay Seasoning (or 1 teaspoon each kosher salt, sweet paprika, and garlic powder)

1 lemon

2 tablespoons unsalted butter

One 10-ounce [283 g] package frozen peas

½ cup [120 ml] half-and-half

½ teaspoon kosher salt

Let some air out of the potato chip bag and then crush the bag with a rolling pin or wine bottle to make fine crumbs. Transfer the potato chip crumbs to a large bowl and add the salmon, ricotta, and Old Bay. Finely grate the zest from the lemon and add it to the bowl (reserve the zested lemon). Stir the mixture well to combine, really breaking up the salmon as you mix.

Divide the mixture into 8 equal portions and use your hands to form each into a patty. It's helpful to divide the mixture in half and then in half again and so on to make sure the patties are the same size.

Place the butter in a large nonstick skillet over medium-high heat. Once it melts and begins to bubble, place the fish cakes in the skillet and cook without disturbing them until their bottoms are nicely browned (what a sentence!), 2 to 3 minutes. Use a spatula to carefully flip each one over and cook until nicely browned on the second side, another 2 to 3 minutes. You might need to cook the fish cakes in 2 batches depending on the size of your pan (you don't want to crowd the pan, and definitely give yourself space to flip them—think of the spacing like pancakes). Transfer the fish cakes to a plate and cover them with foil to keep them warm.

Turn the heat to high and place the peas, half-and-half, and salt in the same skillet. Cook, stirring, just until the peas are bright green and tender and the half-and-half has reduced slightly, about 4 minutes. Transfer the saucy peas to a serving platter and place the fish cakes on top. Cut the zested lemon into wedges and serve the wedges with the fish cakes for squeezing over. Serve immediately.

MUSTARDY CRACKER CRUMB FISH

I started making this fish a couple of years ago during our volunteer shift at Angel Food East (you can read more about this on page 176). Since the fish we get from our county's food bank is only available frozen, I find that it benefits from a little something to perk it up after thawing. This mustardy, buttery cracker crumb mixture is my favorite little something. It's a small something. It's literally crumbs. But it makes a difference and it's a way to express our care for what we're preparing and who we're preparing it for. Serve with a simple salad or a quick slaw made of shredded cabbage that you sprinkle with a little vinegar and salt and scrunch with your hands to soften the cabbage, then add a big spoonful of mayonnaise and a sprinkle of Old Bay Seasoning so that the flavor complements the fish. This also goes well with rice, baked potatoes . . . just about anything. Tartar sauce is also a good accompaniment. For a quick homemade one, finely chop a pickle and a spoonful of capers and mix them with some mayonnaise, a little lemon juice, and lots of freshly ground black pepper.

Serves 4

20 saltine, soda, or Ritz crackers (or 1 cup oyster crackers, 65 g total whichever you use)

2 tablespoons Dijon mustard

2 tablespoons unsalted butter, melted (or olive oil)

½ teaspoon kosher salt

1 teaspoon Old Bay Seasoning (or ½ teaspoon each sweet paprika and garlic powder)

Four 6-ounce [170 g] boneless, skinless, flaky, white-fleshed fish fillets, such as cod or flounder

1 lemon, cut into wedges, for serving

Preheat your oven to 425°F [220°C]. Line a sheet pan with parchment paper.

Place the crackers in a large plastic bag and seal the bag. Crush the crackers with a rolling pin or a wine bottle until the crumbs are very fine.

Place the crushed crackers, mustard, butter, salt, and Old Bay in a bowl and stir well to combine.

Place the fish fillets on the prepared sheet pan. Wet your hands with water and pat equal portions of the cracker mixture into an even layer on top of each piece of fish (wetting your hands makes the spreading easier).

Bake until the cracker mixture is light golden brown and the fish flakes when you nudge it with a fork, about 15 minutes. Serve right away with lemon wedges for squeezing on top.

ARAYES WITH YOGURT SAUCE

Al-Ameer, a renowned Lebanese restaurant in Dearborn, Michigan, is halfway between the Detroit Metro Airport and downtown Detroit. Once when I was visiting Detroit on book tour, I took a morning flight from New York and arrived at the restaurant with my suitcase right in time for lunch. I couldn't decide what to order and my waiter could tell. "Get the arayes," he said. And I'm so glad I did. The grilled, spiced meat–stuffed pitas, which are popular throughout Arab cooking, came with thick, garlicky yogurt and chopped salad and it was just the best lunch ever.

I've looked into lots of recipes ever since, and some feature a large meat-to-pita ratio, while others are much thinner. I like the thinner ones since they remind me so much of Al-Ameer, but also because you get more of a crispy vibe, which is the vibe I'm basically always looking for. To make them, you just fill pita breads with spiced ground meat and grill them (lamb and beef are the most traditional, but I've made them with turkey, too). You can assemble them up to a couple of days in advance, refrigerate them, and then grill them just before serving. Don't have a grill? Just cook them in a hot cast-iron pan slicked with a tiny bit of oil. Serve with a platter of sliced cucumbers spritzed with lemon juice and sprinkled with salt.

Serves 4

For the arayes
1 pound [453 g] lean ground beef, lamb, or turkey

2 garlic cloves, minced

1 teaspoon kosher salt

1 teaspoon freshly ground black pepper

1 teaspoon ground cumin

½ teaspoon ground cinnamon

½ teaspoon ground allspice

Four 6-inch [15-cm] pitas, halved crosswise

Cooking spray (my preference is olive oil spray, but use whatever you have)

For the yogurt sauce
1 cup [240 g] full-fat plain yogurt (regular yogurt, not thick Greek yogurt)

2 garlic cloves, minced

2 tablespoons water

½ teaspoon kosher salt

For serving
1 lemon, cut into wedges

First, make the arayes
Get your outdoor grill going (gas or charcoal) with medium heat (make sure it's truly medium and not too hot) and make sure the grate is super clean.

Place the meat, minced garlic, salt, pepper, cumin, cinnamon, and allspice in a large bowl and use your hands to mix everything together. Evenly divide the meat into 8 equal portions and stuff each pita half with the spiced meat. Press the meat into an even layer so each pita half is an even thickness.

Spray both sides of the arayes with cooking spray. Grill, turning each pita a few times during cooking,

until the pitas are crispy and dark golden brown and the arayes are firm to the touch (this is how you'll know the meat is cooked through), about 7 minutes total.

Next, make the sauce
Place the yogurt, garlic, water, and salt in a small bowl and whisk well to combine. Season to taste with more salt if needed.

And serve
Serve the arayes with the yogurt sauce for dipping and the lemon wedges for squeezing over.

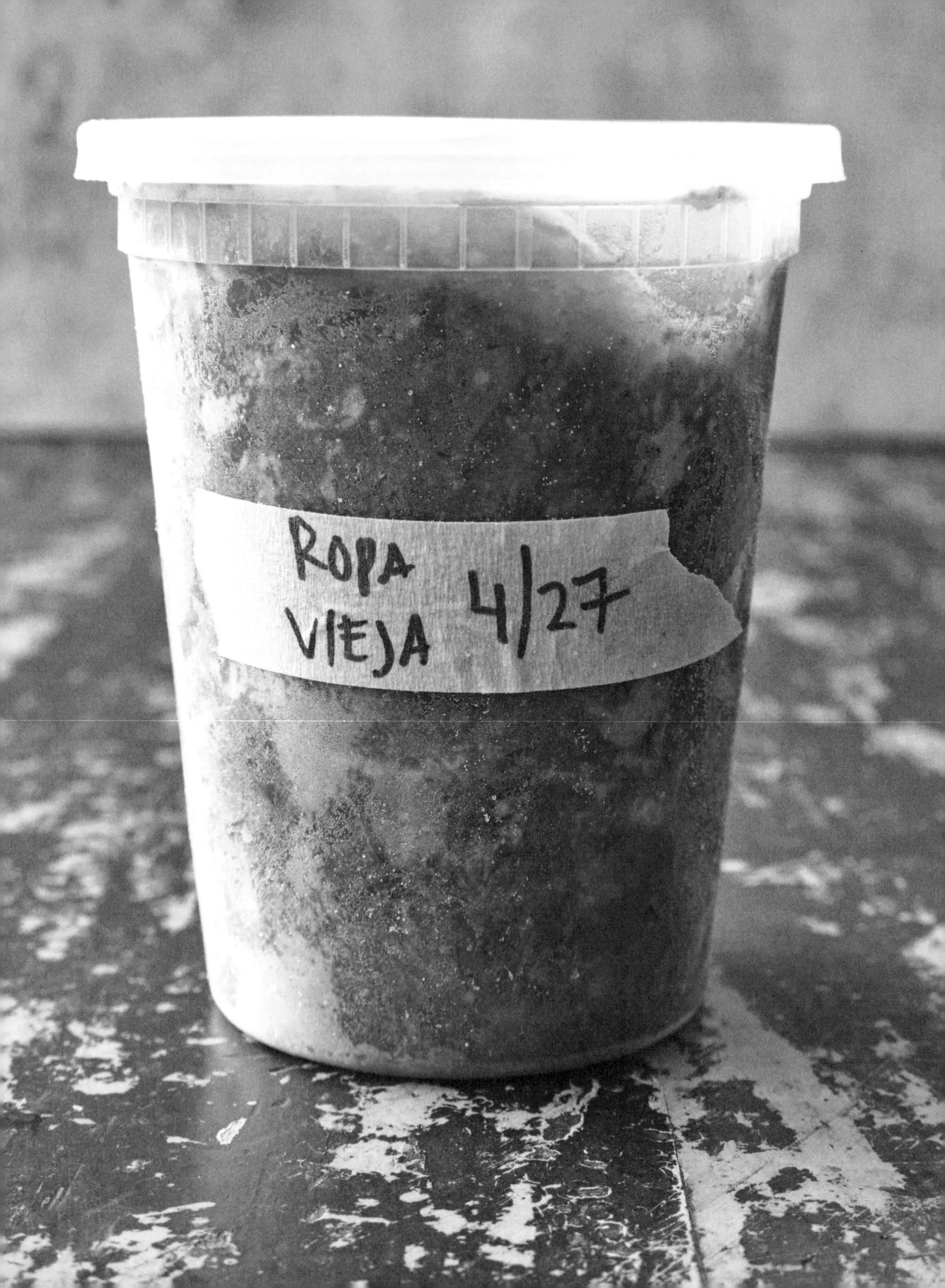
ROPA VIEJA 4/27

2

ELEVEN MAKE-AHEAD MAINS

KALE + MUSHROOM POT PIE

Puffed and golden and impressive, this pot pie is one of the heartiest and most satisfying vegetarian main dishes there ever was. Instead of classic pot pie filling, typically meat-heavy and thickly sauced, this one is packed with vegetables. Roasting the mushrooms and onion gives it an extra layer of flavor, and the shingled puff pastry is just plain fun (plus you don't have to make your own dough or crimp any edges).

Some logistics: you can make the filling up to a few days in advance and refrigerate it; or you could lay the puff pastry on the skillet up to a day in advance, refrigerate it, and then brush with the egg right before baking. A combination of creminis and shiitakes is great here, but feel free to use whatever mushrooms you can find and enjoy.

Serves 4

1½ pounds [680 g] assorted fresh mushrooms, tough stems discarded, roughly chopped

1 large yellow onion, finely chopped

¼ cup [60 ml] extra-virgin olive oil

Kosher salt

½ pound [227 g] kale (any type), tough stems discarded, coarsely chopped (1 standard bunch)

3 large carrots, peeled and finely diced

½ cup [113 g] sour cream

One 5.2-ounce [150 g] package garlic-and-herb Boursin cheese (or goat cheese)

1 teaspoon freshly ground black pepper

1 sheet puff pastry from a frozen package [about 8 ounces (227 g)], thawed

1 large egg, lightly beaten

A large pinch of flaky salt (such as Maldon . . . or just regular salt), for finishing

Preheat your oven to 400°F [200°C].

Place the mushrooms and onion on a sheet pan. Drizzle with the olive oil and sprinkle with 1 teaspoon kosher salt. Use your hands to toss everything together and spread out in an even layer (the vegetables will be packed tightly). Roast, stirring occasionally, until the vegetables are just softened, about 20 minutes. Reserve the mixture.

Bring a medium pot of water to a boil and salt it generously. Add the kale and carrots and cook until they're just tender, about 3 minutes. Drain in a colander and press down to extract all the extra liquid.

Place the sour cream, Boursin cheese, and black pepper in a large bowl and stir well to combine (the cheese might be a little lumpy, and that's okay). Stir in all the vegetables. Season the mixture to taste with salt and transfer it to a 9-inch [23-cm] cast-iron skillet (or other medium ovenproof skillet or a baking dish).

Place the puff pastry sheet on a cutting board and use a chef's knife to cut it into small triangles. Shingle the triangles on top of the pot pie filling.

Use a pastry brush or your fingertips to brush the egg over the surface of the pastry (you probably won't use the entire egg, and that's okay—discard or save for your next omelet). Sprinkle the pie with the flaky salt.

Bake the pie until the pastry is puffed up and dark brown, about 30 minutes. Serve hot.

VEGETARIAN MUFFULETTAS WITH PICKLED ICEBERG

Traditionally filled with lots of cured Italian meats and cheeses, muffulleta sandwiches are as iconic to New Orleans as Leah Chase's gumbo. This vegetarian version has the spirit of the original, but is its own thing. The pickled iceberg leaves remind me that meat isn't always required to make a sandwich substantial and well-spiced. Feel free to put some thinly sliced cucumbers or onions in the leftover brine and store in a jar in your refrigerator for up to a week.

Makes 4

For the pickled iceberg
½ cup [120 ml] red wine vinegar

1 cup [240 ml] water

3 garlic cloves, minced

1 tablespoon granulated sugar

1 tablespoon fennel seeds

1 tablespoon dried oregano

1 teaspoon pimentón (smoked Spanish paprika)

2 teaspoons kosher salt

1 medium head iceberg lettuce, ragged outer leaves and core discarded, remaining leaves separated

For the sandwiches
½ cup [120 g] pimento-stuffed green olives, finely chopped

1 tablespoon capers

⅓ cup [80 g] mayonnaise

4 individual sandwich rolls (preferably with sesame seeds on top), halved horizontally

¼ pound [113 g] thinly sliced aged provolone cheese

One 7-ounce [198 g] jar roasted red peppers, drained, rinsed, and patted dry with a paper towel

½ pound [227 g] fresh mozzarella cheese, thinly sliced

First, make the pickled iceberg
Place the vinegar, water, garlic, sugar, fennel seeds, oregano, pimentón, and salt in a small saucepan over high heat. Bring the mixture to a boil, stir to dissolve the sugar and salt, and then turn off the heat.

Working with 1 leaf at a time, place the lettuce into a large bowl and pour a little of the hot brine on each leaf as you layer them in the bowl. Pour any extra brine into the bowl. Let the mixture cool to room temperature (at this point you can cover the bowl in plastic and refrigerate it for up to a day). Once the brine cools, drain the iceberg (save the brine for another use or discard) and pat dry the leaves with a kitchen towel.

Next, finish the sandwiches
While the lettuce is cooling down, stir together the olives, capers, and mayonnaise in a small bowl.

Divide the olive mixture between the tops and bottoms of each roll. Layer each sandwich evenly with provolone, peppers, pickled iceberg, and mozzarella. Close each sandwich and wrap each one tightly in plastic wrap.

Place a flat surface (like a cutting board or sheet pan) on top of the sandwiches and put something heavy on top (like a cast-iron skillet or a few cans of beans). Let the sandwiches sit for at least 1 hour at room temperature (or a day in the refrigerator, but bring to room temperature before serving).

Unwrap the sandwiches, cut each in half, and serve.

RATATOUILLE + RICOTTA BAKED PASTA

This pasta includes way more vegetables than pasta, a whopping four-to-one ratio to be exact. You can use any type of short pasta for this (meaning not only any shape from gemelli to rotini, but also any type from regular to whole wheat to gluten-free). You can roast the vegetables up to three days ahead of time, or make the whole recipe up until the point of baking the pasta and cover it in the fridge for up to two days before baking. I love using a sheet pan to bake the pasta because you get lots of crispy edges (plus you can reuse one of the pans you roasted the vegetables on, saving you some cleanup). Try grinding extra fennel seeds with salt (using a mortar and pestle or a food processor or a coffee grinder) and sprinkle the mixture on your next roast chicken, pork, or squash. Game changer.

Serves 6

2 red, yellow, and/or orange bell peppers, stemmed, seeded, and cut into 1-inch [2.5-cm] pieces

2 pounds [907 g] zucchini (about 5 medium), ends discarded, cut into 1-inch [2.5-cm] pieces

1 large eggplant [about 1 pound (453 g)], ends discarded, cut into 1-inch [2.5-cm] pieces

12 ounces [340 g] cherry tomatoes (1 pint)

6 tablespoons extra-virgin olive oil, divided

2 teaspoons dried oregano, divided

2 teaspoons fennel seeds (optional), divided

Kosher salt

1 pound [453 g] short pasta (such as rotini, gemelli, or ziti)

16 ounces [453 g] whole milk ricotta cheese

1 cup [110 g] finely grated Parmesan cheese

Preheat your oven to 425°F [220°C].

Set a large pot of water to boil.

Divide the peppers, zucchini, eggplant, and tomatoes between 2 sheet pans. Drizzle each with 3 tablespoons olive oil and sprinkle each with 1 teaspoon dried oregano, 1 teaspoon fennel seeds (if using), and 1 teaspoon salt. Mix everything together with your hands and spread out into even layers. Roast the sheets of vegetables, giving them a stir after 15 minutes, until the vegetables are softened, about 30 minutes.

Meanwhile, salt the boiling water generously and cook the pasta 1 minute less than the package

instructs. Drain the pasta in a colander. Return it to the now-empty pot and add the roasted vegetables, and ricotta cheese. Mix everything well to combine and season to taste with salt (don't be shy, it might need a couple of teaspoons, if not a full tablespoon—you're seasoning a lot of food here!).

Transfer the mixture to one of the sheet pans you roasted the vegetables on and spread it out in an even layer. Evenly sprinkle the Parmesan cheese on top.

Roast until the Parmesan is melted and browned, about 20 minutes. Serve hot.

STREET FAIR STUFFED MUSHROOMS

Filled with sausage and peppers, my favorite thing to eat at a street fair, these stuffed mushrooms are a fun dinner. A few tips. One: use scissors to roughly chop the arugula directly in the package it comes in. Two: use any type of sausage here, whether traditional pork or turkey, chicken, or even a vegan sausage. Three: make these ahead! The stuffed mushrooms can hang in the refrigerator for a day or two before you pop them in the oven to finish cooking before serving. Note that this recipe makes enough for two per person, which is good for a main dish, but you could get away with one per person if it was part of a bigger spread, perhaps a tray of Ratatouille + Ricotta Baked Pasta (page 28) and a big green salad. You could also turn this into a fun nosh by stuffing the mixture into creminis (which are just baby portobellos). Leftovers can be simply warmed and enjoyed, or you can chop them up and toss them with hot pasta.

Serves 4

8 large portobello mushrooms, stems discarded, cleaned

2 tablespoons extra-virgin olive oil

1 pound [453 g] sweet or hot Italian sausage, casings discarded

2 red, yellow, and/or orange bell peppers, stemmed, seeded, and finely chopped

1 large red onion, finely chopped

2 tablespoons tomato paste

4 garlic cloves, minced

5 ounces [141 g] fresh baby arugula, roughly chopped

½ cup [35 g] fine dried breadcrumbs

Kosher salt

4 ounces [113 g] goat cheese, crumbled

Preheat your oven to 425°F [220°C].

Line a sheet pan with parchment paper or aluminum foil (this will make cleanup easier) and then set a cooling rack on top. Place the mushroom caps, gill side up, on the rack. When the mushrooms cook later and release their liquid, this rack will keep them from sitting in it. Hang onto the tray of mushrooms and move along with your filling.

Place the olive oil in a large, heavy pot (like a Dutch oven) over medium heat. Use your hands to break the sausage into small pieces directly into the pot. Cook, stirring now and then to break up the pieces so they're quite small, until the sausage fat is rendered and the meaty bits are beginning to crisp, about 10 minutes. Add the bell peppers and onion and cook, stirring now and then, until the vegetables are softened, about 10 minutes.

Turn off the heat and stir in the tomato paste, garlic, and arugula. The arugula will look like a ton, but just keep stirring and it will wilt and you'll think "where did all of that arugula go?" That's a good thing! Stir in the breadcrumbs. Season the mixture to taste with salt (the exact amount will depend on how salty the sausage is).

Evenly divide the filling among the mushroom caps. Divide the goat cheese among the stuffed mushrooms, dotting the top of each mushroom with the cheese.

Roast the mushrooms until they're tender and the goat cheese is melted and browned, about 20 minutes. Serve warm.

ROGER'S JAMBALAYA

Roger joined our shift at Angel Food East after he retired from teaching and has become a trusted team member and a friend. He's easygoing and is always game to do whatever needs doing in the kitchen. An avid musician, Roger plays and studies Creole music and brings his knowledge of all things Louisiana to the meals we prepare. His jambalaya is a favorite at Angel Food East since it's a comforting one-pot meal that's full of depth. Plus it depends on affordable ingredients (the shrimp are optional), stretches a little meat into a big pot of food (in fact, you can skip the chicken and it's still great with just sausage), and it comes together quickly. It also is just fine to make ahead and reheat later (just set it over low heat and add a splash of water or stock if it needs to loosen up a bit). All of these qualities that make it great for our community also make it a wonderful thing to make at home. Thanks to Roger for showing me, and all of us, how he makes it. Note that it definitely has a little kick, so leave out the cayenne if you don't like things too hot (or add more if you like them extra hot!).

Serves 4

1 pound [453 g] boneless, skinless chicken thighs, cut into 1-inch [2.5-cm] cubes

1 teaspoon kosher salt, plus more as needed

1 teaspoon freshly ground black pepper

1 teaspoon dried red chile powder (ground ancho or chipotle are my favorites, but use whatever you have)

½ teaspoon ground cayenne pepper

2 tablespoons extra-virgin olive oil

½ pound [227 g] smoked andouille sausage, cut into thin coins

1 large yellow onion, finely chopped

2 large celery stalks, finely chopped

2 green bell peppers, stemmed, seeded, and finely chopped

6 garlic cloves, minced

2 tablespoons tomato paste

One 14.5-ounce [411 g] can diced tomatoes with their juice

3 cups [720 ml] chicken stock (homemade, store-bought, or bouillon paste dissolved in boiling water)

1 cup [200 g] long-grain white rice

½ pound [227 g] medium shrimp, peeled and deveined (optional)

A large handful thinly sliced scallions, for serving

Place the chicken in a large bowl and sprinkle with the salt, black pepper, chile powder, and cayenne. Mix everything together and let the chicken sit at room temperature while you cook the sausage.

Place the olive oil in a large, heavy pot (like a Dutch oven) over medium heat. Add the sausage and cook, stirring now and then, until its fat has rendered and it's crisp in spots, about 7 minutes. Use a slotted spoon to transfer the sausage to

a bowl (leave the fat in the pot) and add the seasoned chicken to the pot. Cook the chicken, stirring now and then, until it's browned in spots and just cooked through, about 8 minutes. Use that same slotted spoon to transfer it to the bowl with the sausage.

Add the onion, celery, and bell peppers to the pot and cook, stirring now and then, until they're just softened, about 10 minutes.

(continued)

Add the garlic and tomato paste and cook, stirring, until very fragrant, just a minute. Add the diced tomatoes along with their juice and the chicken stock. Turn the heat to high, bring the mixture to a boil, and then turn it to low. Taste the mixture and season with salt as needed.

Stir in the reserved sausage and chicken and the rice. Cover and cook just until the rice is tender, about 20 minutes.

Uncover the pot, stir in the shrimp (if using), and then cover the pot, turn off the heat, and let the jambalaya sit for 10 minutes so the shrimp cook through from the residual heat and the rice has time to really soak everything in. Serve the jambalaya hot with scallions sprinkled on top.

ROGER + HIS ACCORDION, 2020

TURKEY SHEPHERD'S PIE

While it's often wise to leave classics alone, I can't help but shake things up a bit. The shepherd's pie that follows, a riff on one of my favorite childhood meals, uses ground turkey and stretches the meat with lots of fresh carrots and frozen peas and the whole thing gets topped with a silky puree made mostly of cauliflower with a little potato for heft. If you don't have a food processor to whiz the cauliflower topping together, just mash it all by hand. It might not be silky, but it'll still be great. You can assemble the entire pie a few days in advance and bake just before serving, or you can bake the whole thing in advance and then warm it in a 350°F [175°C] oven until it's piping hot. If you have some fresh thyme or rosemary on hand, mince it up and add it to the turkey while it's cooking.

Serves 4

For the filling

Kosher salt

2 large carrots, peeled and finely diced

One 10-ounce [283 g] package frozen peas

3 tablespoons extra-virgin olive oil, divided

1 pound [453 g] ground turkey (preferably dark meat, but white meat works, too)

1 small yellow onion, finely diced

2 garlic cloves, minced

2 tablespoons all-purpose flour

2 tablespoons tomato paste

1 cup [240 ml] chicken stock (homemade, store-bought, or bouillon paste dissolved in boiling water)

1 tablespoon Worcestershire sauce

For the topping

1 small cauliflower [about 2 pounds (907 g)], outer leaves and core discarded, cut into large florets

1 large baking potato [about ¾ pound (340 g)], peeled and roughly chopped

4 large garlic cloves, peeled (just leave them whole)

¼ cup [60 ml] half-and-half

2 tablespoons unsalted butter

Kosher salt

1 cup [110 g] coarsely grated sharp cheddar cheese

First, preheat your oven to 400°F [200°C].

Next, make the filling
Bring a large pot of water to a boil and salt it generously. Add the carrots and cook until barely tender, about 4 minutes. Add the peas and cook until just bright green, about 30 seconds. Use a handheld strainer or a slotted spoon to transfer the vegetables to a large bowl (leave the boiling water in the pot and save it for your cauliflower topping, which you'll get to in a little while).

Place 2 tablespoons of the olive oil in a medium cast-iron skillet [about 9 inches (23 cm) in diameter, or another ovenproof skillet]. Add the turkey, season generously with salt, and cook, stirring now and then, until all of its moisture evaporates and it's browned in spots, about 10 minutes. Transfer the browned turkey to the bowl with the carrots and peas.

Add the remaining 1 tablespoon oil to the skillet and add the onion. Cook, stirring now and then,

(continued)

until the onion begins to soften, about 6 minutes. Season with a large pinch of salt. Add the garlic, flour, and tomato paste. Cook, stirring, until everything is fragrant and well-incorporated, about 1 minute. While stirring, slowly pour in the chicken stock and then the Worcestershire sauce. Bring the mixture to a boil, turn the heat to low, and simmer for just a minute to let some of the raw flour taste cook off. Turn off the heat.

Scrape the onion mixture into the bowl with the turkey, carrots, and peas and mix well to combine. Season the mixture to taste with salt. Return the mixture to the skillet (it's easier to mix it in the bowl) and hang onto it.

Next, make the topping

Return the pot of vegetable water to a boil and add the cauliflower, potato, and garlic cloves. Boil until the vegetables are very tender (test with a paring knife), about 15 minutes. Drain them in a colander and give them a good shake to make sure all the excess water goes down the drain.

Transfer vegetables to the bowl of a food processor along with the half-and-half, butter, and 1 teaspoon salt. Puree until smooth and season to taste with more salt if needed.

Finish the pie

Cover the surface of the turkey mixture with the cauliflower mash and then sprinkle the cheese on top. Roast the pie until the cheese is melted and browned in spots, 25 to 30 minutes. Serve hot.

FRENCH ONION MEATLOAF

My Aunt Debby was one of my favorite people. We went from being merely related to being friends when I was in high school and we started going out to lunch, which we continued to do until she passed away a few years ago. Over our nearly two decades of meals together, she introduced me to things like the art of ordering two appetizers instead of an entrée (it leaves more room for dessert) and the joy of a great piece of gossip.

On the incredibly rare occasions she cooked, the only thing she ever made was meatloaf with a packet of dried onion soup mix in it to flavor it. This recipe, filled with slowly caramelized onions and cubes of Gruyère, is inspired by hers. I think she would've loved it and I hope you do, too. Note that the onions take a full 45 minutes to cook, but you can prepare them up to a week in advance.

Serves 6–8

2 tablespoons extra-virgin olive oil

2 tablespoons unsalted butter

3 large yellow onions, finely diced (about 1 ¼ pounds [567 g], or about 4 cups diced)

Kosher salt

¼ cup [60 ml] Worcestershire sauce

2 tablespoons balsamic vinegar

2 large eggs

1 cup [70 g] panko breadcrumbs

2 pounds [907 g] ground turkey

One 7-ounce [198g] block Gruyère cheese, cut into ½-inch [1 cm] cubes (nearly 2 cups diced)

Preheat your oven to 350°F [175°c]. Line a sheet pan with parchment paper.

Place the oil and butter in a heavy saucepan or Dutch oven (something that will conduct heat evenly) and set it over high heat. Once the butter melts and sizzles, add the onions and cook, stirring now and then, until everything is sizzling together, about 5 minutes. Sprinkle the onions with 1 teaspoon kosher salt and turn the heat to medium. Continue to cook the onions, stirring now and then and adjusting the heat as needed to keep them from burning and/or sticking, until the onions have melted into a dark brown, amazing-smelling heap, almost like an onion jam, 40 minutes. They will have cooked down to about a third of their original volume. Add the Worcestershire sauce and balsamic vinegar, turn the heat to high and bring the mixture just to a boil, then turn off the heat. Let the onions cool to room temperature.

Place the eggs and 2 teaspoons kosher salt in a large bowl and whisk well to combine. Add the cooled onion mixture and the breadcrumbs and stir well to combine. Add the turkey and diced cheese and use your (clean!) hands to mix everything together.

Transfer the mixture to the prepared sheet pan and shape into a 10-by-5-inch [25-by-13-cm] rectangle that's about 2 inches [5 cm] tall.

Bake the meatloaf until it's dark brown, firm to the touch, the bits of exposed cheese are bubbling, and the meatloaf measures 165F° [74°C] on a digital thermometer inserted at its center, about 1 hour. Note that this is not the most attractive thing in the world, so don't despair (also note that it's delicious).

Serve in thick slices hot, warm, or cold in a sandwich (my personal favorite).

SHREDDED PORK IN THE SPIRIT OF COCHINITA PIBIL

A few years ago, I had one of the best lunches I've ever experienced at El Compadre, a restaurant in Philadelphia's Italian Market neighborhood, with my friend Lacey. It's closed now, but when we went, it was run by Cristina Martínez and her husband, Ben Miller, who famously run South Philly Barbacoa (you might be familiar with Cristina and her story from Netflix's *Chef's Table*). An outspoken advocate for immigrants' rights, Cristina gathers and empowers her community through her cooking. Over chiles relleños and cochinita pibil, Lacey and I got to feel the warmth of her hospitality up close and personal.

Cochinita pibil, the Yucatán Peninsula's signature slow-cooked pork, is traditionally prepared a lot like the lamb barbacoa that Cristina is righteously beloved for. It starts with digging a pit in the ground.

The version that follows is hardly authentic. But it's really delicious and could not be easier to make. You need little more than a heavy pot and some patience. Once the pork is cooked and shredded, it can be stored in a container in the refrigerator for up to a week, warmed over low heat in a saucepan, or crisped in a non-stick skillet. Enjoy it on its own alongside some rice and beans, or tuck it into tacos, quesadillas, burritos, or pressed sandwiches. The achiote paste (made its brilliant red hue by annatto seeds) and chiles de árbol are widely available in grocery stores (look in the aisle with Mexican ingredients). If you can't find one or both of those ingredients, throw in a couple of canned chipotle peppers in adobo sauce. It won't be exactly the same, but it will still be very good.

Serves 6 to 8

One 3-pound [1.4-kg] boneless pork shoulder roast (or pork butt or Boston butt), trimmed of any large pieces of fat or gristle, cut into 4 even pieces

Kosher salt

2 teaspoons freshly ground black pepper

2 teaspoons ground cumin

4 dried bay leaves

8 garlic cloves, crushed

8 dried chiles de árbol (optional)

2 juice oranges, halved

3 tablespoons achiote paste (optional)

¼ cup [60 ml] distilled white vinegar (or fresh lime juice)

¼ cup [60 ml] water

Preheat your oven to 300°F [150°C].

Sprinkle the pork pieces all over with 2 teaspoons salt, the pepper, and the cumin. Place them in a large, heavy ovenproof pot (such as a Dutch oven) and tuck in the bay leaves, garlic cloves, and dried chiles (if using). Squeeze the juice from the orange halves over everything and then tuck the squeezed halves right into the pot. Place the achiote paste in a small bowl with the vinegar and water, whisk together, and then pour the mixture into the pot. Cover tightly with a lid or aluminum foil.

Roast the pork until it's incredibly tender and shreds easily when you poke at it with a couple of forks, about 3 hours. Use those forks to shred the pork directly in the pot (discard any large pieces of fat as you work). Mix the shredded pork together with all the juices in the pot and season to taste with salt (don't be shy with the salt). You can toss the oranges, but you could also enjoy them (they're totally edible). Serve warm.

RASCAL HOUSE STUFFED CABBAGE

Wolfie Cohen's Rascal House was a huge restaurant near where my great-grandmother spent the final years of her life in Miami, Florida. Vast and energetic, going to the Rascal House felt like walking into the dining room from *Dirty Dancing*. Filled with older Jewish New Yorkers who had decamped to Florida (or who, like my family, were there visiting those relatives), the Rascal House was known for its huge portions, huge menus, and huge baskets of rolls and buckets of half-sour pickles. To this day I can picture the waitresses in their uniforms and hear the sound of booths of families (the whole mishpocheh!) kvetching and kvelling.

I'm sad to say the Rascal House is no longer there, but its feeling, its zeitgeist, looms large in families like mine and in foods like this stuffed cabbage, straight from the old country via New York via Florida. Here's my version, on the lighter side with ground turkey and brown rice, but still full of flavor and spirit. You can make the filling, sauce, and blanched cabbage leaves up to a few days ahead of time and then assemble and bake just before serving. Or assemble everything up to a day ahead and bake just before serving. Or (!) you can bake the whole thing, cool it down, refrigerate for up to a day or two, and then just warm before serving. It's very forgiving.

Serves 4

For the sauce

2 tablespoons extra-virgin olive oil

1 medium yellow onion, thinly sliced into half moons

3 garlic cloves, minced

One 28-ounce [794 g] can crushed tomatoes

3 tablespoons red wine vinegar

3 tablespoons light brown sugar

1 teaspoon kosher salt

For the cabbage

Kosher salt

1 small head Savoy cabbage [about 1 pound (453 g); if you can't find one that small, no worries, I'll walk you through what to do with it]

1 pound [453 g] ground turkey (preferably dark meat, but white meat works, too)

2 large eggs, lightly beaten

1½ cups [210 g] cooked brown rice

¼ teaspoon ground allspice

3 tablespoons minced fresh dill

⅓ cup [65 g] raisins (optional)

First, preheat your oven to 350°F [175°C].

Next, make the sauce
Place the olive oil in a medium saucepan over medium heat. Add the onion and cook, stirring now and then, until just softened, about 8 minutes. Add the garlic and cook until fragrant, about 30 seconds. Add the crushed tomatoes with their juice and turn the heat to high. Bring to a boil, turn the heat to low, and stir in the vinegar, brown

sugar, and 1 teaspoon salt. Simmer the sauce until the tomatoes lose their tin-can taste, about 20 minutes. Turn off the heat and reserve the sauce.

Then, prepare the cabbage
Bring a large pot of water to a boil and salt it generously. While it's coming to a boil, cut off and discard a small slice at the base of the cabbage and discard any blemished outer leaves. Separate the large cabbage leaves from the stem, slicing off

(continued)

more at the base as you go to loosen the leaves. Cut out and discard the ribs from each leaf. You want a pile of about a dozen large cabbage leaves. You will end up making 8 pieces of stuffed cabbage and the largest leaves will work for most of them, but it's good to have a few extra for patchwork.

If you have a lot more cabbage left at the center of the cabbage (looking almost like a small cabbage), you can save it for another use (check out the More-Vegetable-than-Rice Fried Rice on page 58 or the Old-School Borscht on page 111, or just make slaw!). Or you can finely chop it, toss it with a little olive oil and salt, and then put it in a large baking dish and use it as a bed for the stuffed cabbage rolls that you're about to make. It will roast and soften along with the rolls and just offer you a little extra something.

Back to the stuffed cabbage. Place the large cabbage leaves in the boiling water and push them down to submerge them. Cook until they're just softened, about 4 minutes. Drain the cabbage in a colander and rinse with cool water. Place the leaves on a kitchen towel to dry them (and really pat them dry, too, as the drier they are, the less soggy your stuffed cabbage will be).

Place the ground turkey, eggs, rice, allspice, dill, raisins (if using), and 2 teaspoons salt in a large bowl. Mix well to combine (your hands are the best tool for the job).

Evenly divide the filling into 8 portions. Lay down as many large cabbage leaves as can fit onto your work surface. Place a portion of filling on each one and then roll each as if it were a small burrito, tucking in the sides as you roll. Repeat the process to make 8 cabbage rolls. If any piece of cabbage isn't large enough, just use one of your extra blanched leaves. These do not have to be perfect, just snug.

Place the cabbage rolls, seam side down, in a baking dish (if you chopped extra cabbage and already put it in the baking dish, just put the stuffed cabbage rolls on top of it). Evenly pour the tomato sauce over the cabbage rolls. Cover the baking dish with aluminum foil and bake until the sauce is bubbling and the cabbage rolls are firm to the touch (letting you know the turkey is cooked through), about 50 minutes. Serve hot.

EIGHTH AVENUE ROPA VIEJA

In my early twenties, I ended up living in a studio apartment in the same building that I grew up in. It was a surreal experience, almost a time loop, and living there allowed me to reconnect to some of the places I went to as a little kid. One of those places was La Taza del Oro, down the block on Eighth Avenue, a very special lunch counter that opened in 1947 and sadly closed in 2015. Along with Casa Adela in the East Village, La Taza del Oro was one of New York's iconic Puerto Rican restaurants and it served dishes from other cultures too, including traditional Cuban ropa vieja (which translates to "old clothes," an evocative description of the texture of the shredded beef).

I make this version at home regularly, and while it doesn't bring back a restaurant I wish was still thriving, it helps me keep my memories of it alive. It's also just so satisfying and soul-warming (which is why I made it a few times for our local volunteer EMT squad when Covid-19 hit our area).

After cooking, shred the beef and store in a container in the refrigerator for up to a week (it's honestly better the longer it sits). Warm it up in a saucepan over low heat (splash with a little water or stock if it needs some moisture) and then enjoy on its own with rice or sweet, starchy things like roasted squash, fried plantains, grilled corn, or Sweet + Spicy Mashed Sweet Potatoes (page 135). It's especially great with the Best Black Beans with Avocado Salad (page 62). You could also use this beef for tacos or inside of a pressed sandwich (try it on your next grilled cheese).

Serves 6 to 8

1 large yellow onion, thinly sliced into half moons

6 garlic cloves, crushed

2 medium green bell peppers, stemmed, seeded, and thinly sliced

One 14.5-ounce [411 g] can diced tomatoes with their juice

¼ cup [60 ml] yellow mustard

⅓ cup [65 g] raisins

½ cup [120 g] pimento-stuffed green olives, plus 3 tablespoons olive brine for finishing the dish

One 2- to 3-pound [907 g to 1.3 kg] boneless chuck roast, trimmed of any large pieces of fat or gristle, cut into 3 even pieces

2 teaspoons kosher salt

1 teaspoon freshly ground black pepper

2 teaspoons ground cumin

Fresh cilantro, for serving (optional)

Preheat your oven to 300°F [150°C].

Place the onion, garlic, bell peppers, diced tomatoes with their juice, mustard, raisins, and olives (hang onto that brine for later) in a large, heavy ovenproof pot (such as a Dutch oven). Mix well to combine.

Sprinkle the chuck roast pieces all over with the salt, black pepper, and cumin. Nestle the pieces into the mixture in the pot. Cover the pot tightly with a lid or aluminum foil.

Roast the beef until it's incredibly tender and shreds easily when you poke at it with tongs or a couple of forks, about 3 hours. Add the olive brine to the pot and use those tongs or forks to shred the beef directly in the pot (discard any large pieces of fat as you work) and mix it together with the juices. Season to taste with salt. Serve warm with cilantro sprinkled on top (if you'd like).

SHEET PAN LAMB MEATBALLS WITH SWEET + SOUR EGGPLANT

Grace, who isn't the biggest fan of lamb or eggplant, loves this recipe, which I take as a major endorsement. You roast cubes of eggplant (no messy frying!) and then toss them with a tomato paste and red wine vinegar mixture that's just barely sweetened with sugar. While the eggplant roasts, you mix ground lamb with garlic, a couple of spices, and salt, and then roll that into little meatballs. Everything gets one final roast together and then gets showered with feta cheese and, voilà, dinner. You can make the whole thing up until the point of adding the feta up to a day ahead and just wrap in foil and then warm in a 300°F [150°C] oven for about 15 minutes or so. Or you can roast the eggplant ahead and then finish the whole thing just before serving. This goes well with couscous (try the Palm Springs Pearl Couscous + Citrus Salad, page 128) or buttered rice; it's also nice next to cooked greens, a big salad, warm pita bread, and/or Grace's Green Beans with Garlic + Tomatoes (page 131).

Serves 4

For the eggplant

2 pounds [907 g] eggplant (about 2 medium), ends trimmed, cut into bite-sized pieces

¼ cup [60 ml] extra-virgin olive oil

1 teaspoon kosher salt

For the sauce

1 cup [240 ml] water

¼ cup [60 ml] tomato paste

1 tablespoon granulated sugar

1 tablespoon red wine vinegar

½ teaspoon kosher salt

For the meatballs

1 pound [453 g] ground lamb

4 garlic cloves, minced

1 teaspoon ground cumin

½ teaspoon ground cinnamon

1 teaspoon kosher salt

To serve

½ cup [55 g] crumbled feta cheese

1 small handful fresh soft herbs (such as parsley, chives, mint, and/or cilantro), chopped (a little stem is fine and these are optional)

First, preheat your oven to 425°F [220°C].

Next, roast the eggplant
Place the eggplant on a sheet pan and drizzle with the olive oil. Sprinkle with the 1 teaspoon salt and use your hands to mix everything together and then spread the eggplant out in an even layer. Roast, stirring now and then, until softened and browned in spots, about 30 minutes. While the eggplant's in the oven, get your sauce and your meatball mixtures sorted.

Meanwhile, make the sauce
Place the water, tomato paste, sugar, vinegar, and ½ teaspoon salt in a small bowl and whisk together. Hang onto it.

Next, make the meatballs
Place the lamb, garlic, cumin, cinnamon, and 1 teaspoon salt in a large bowl. Use your hands to mix everything together. Form the mixture into 20 even portions. It's helpful to divide the mixture in half and then in half again and so on to make

sure the meatballs are the same size. Wetting your hands with cold water will help keep the mixture from sticking to them. Roll each into a small ball.

Sauce the eggplant and roast the meatballs
Once the eggplant is roasted, pour the sauce mixture over it and stir everything together using two large spoons (like you were mixing a salad). Be sure to scrape the bottom of the sheet pan to release any stuck bits of eggplant.

Evenly space the meatballs on top of the eggplant mixture and roast until they're firm to the touch and browned on top, about 15 minutes.

To serve
Transfer the meatballs and eggplant to a serving dish (or just serve straight from the sheet pan). Sprinkle the feta and herbs on top. Serve immediately.

3

—

ELEVEN VEGAN ONE-POT MEALS FOR EVERYONE

BEST VEGAN CHILI

Pressed, crumbled, seasoned tofu gives you the texture and feeling of ground meat in this vegan chili, and the little bit of cornmeal at the end thickens it (while keeping it gluten-free if that's important to you!), which makes it feel extra substantial. Don't be scared off by the large quantity of ground spices that go into the tofu. They will eventually flavor the entire pot of chili, not just the tofu. Serve with toppings like hot sauce, lime wedges, fresh chopped fresh cilantro, and/or diced white onion. Sour cream and cheese are both nice if you're not vegan, and vegan versions of those are nice, too. You can also stretch out the chili with tortilla chips, rice, cornbread, baked potatoes, or, for the best vegan chili dogs, use it to top vegan hot dogs.

Serves 4 to 6

One 14-ounce [397 g] container extra-firm tofu, drained

¼ cup [60 ml] extra-virgin olive oil, plus 2 extra tablespoons for the vegetables

Kosher salt

1 tablespoon garlic powder

1 tablespoon ground cumin

1 tablespoon pimentón (smoked Spanish paprika)

1 tablespoon red chile powder (ground ancho or chipotle are my favorites, but use whatever you have)

1 large yellow onion, finely diced

1 red bell pepper, stemmed, seeded, and finely diced

6 garlic cloves, minced

One 15-ounce [425 g] can red kidney beans, rinsed and drained

One 15-ounce [425 g] can black beans, rinsed and drained

One 28-ounce [794 g] can diced tomatoes with their juice

3 tablespoons yellow cornmeal

Wrap the tofu in a clean kitchen towel. Put a cutting board on top of the tofu and then put something heavy, like a Dutch oven, on top of that and let it sit for at least 15 minutes. Pressing it will help remove excess moisture.

And here's where I break my own rules. This is a one-pot meal chapter, but this recipe is so much easier to clean up after if you use a nonstick skillet to cook the tofu and then transfer it to a large pot later with everything else. I'm sorry if I misled you, but this is the only exception to the one-pot rule and it's really worth it!

Place the ¼ cup [60 ml] olive oil in a large nonstick skillet over high heat. Once it's nice and hot, crumble in the tofu so it's roughly the size of beans, and cook it—without stirring!—until it's a little browned and crisp on the bottom, about 4 minutes. Sprinkle the tofu with 2 teaspoons salt, the garlic powder, cumin, pimentón, and chile powder. Cook, stirring, until it's very fragrant,

about 1 minute. Take the skillet off the heat and hang onto it.

Place a heavy pot (like a Dutch oven) over medium-low heat and add the remaining 2 tablespoons olive oil along with the onion and bell pepper. Cook, stirring now and then, until the vegetables begin to soften, about 8 minutes. Stir in the in the garlic and cook until just fragrant, about 30 seconds.

Add the reserved tofu to the pot along with the kidney beans, black beans, tomatoes with their juice, and the cornmeal. Fill one of the bean cans with water and add the water to the pot (saves you a measuring cup!). Scrape the bottom of the pot with a wooden spoon to loosen any flavorful bits that might be stuck there. Bring the mixture to a boil, then turn the heat to low and simmer, stirring the chili every so often, until thick and rich, about 25 minutes. Season the chili to taste with salt if needed. Serve hot.

BLACK BEAN + CORN TAMALE PIE

Efficient! Little cleanup! Comforting! This recipe is all of my favorite things. If you want something a little fresh and green alongside, serve with a green salad topped with lots of avocado. You can double the lime and vegan mayonnaise mixture and use it to dress the salad. If you use chopped cilantro in the cornbread topping, go ahead and chop a little extra for sprinkling on top of each serving (this looks really nice, but is not required!).

Serve 4

For the topping

½ cup [120 ml] water

2 tablespoons chia seeds

3 tablespoons extra-virgin olive oil

1 cup [240 ml] non-dairy milk of your choice

2 tablespoons apple cider vinegar

2 teaspoons baking powder

2 teaspoons kosher salt

¾ cup [105 g] whole wheat flour

¾ cup [105 g] yellow cornmeal

1 large handful fresh cilantro, finely chopped (optional, but if you use it, a little stem is fine)

For the filling

2 tablespoons extra-virgin olive oil

1 large yellow onion, finely chopped

1 red bell pepper, stemmed, seeded, and finely chopped

3 tablespoons tomato paste

4 garlic cloves, minced

2 teaspoons ground cumin

2 teaspoons pimentón (smoked Spanish paprika)

2 teaspoons kosher salt

One 14.5-ounce [411 g] can diced tomatoes with their juice

One 15-ounce [425 g] can black beans, rinsed and drained

Kernels from 3 ears fresh corn [or a 16-ounce (453 g) package frozen corn kernels]

3 tablespoons nutritional yeast (optional)

For the sauce

½ cup [120 g] vegan mayonnaise

2 tablespoons fresh lime juice

½ teaspoon kosher salt

First, preheat your oven to 425°F [220°C].

Next, make your topping
Place the water in a large bowl with the chia seeds, stir well to combine, and let sit until the chia seeds swell and soften, about 5 minutes.

Once the chia is softened, whisk in the olive oil, non-dairy milk, vinegar, baking powder, and salt. Switch to a spoon and stir in the flour, cornmeal, and cilantro (if using). Hang onto this mixture.

Next, make your filling
Place the olive oil into a large, heavy ovenproof skillet [measuring at least 10 inches (25 cm) wide] over medium heat. Add the onion and bell pepper. Cook, stirring now and then, until just barely softened, about 6 minutes. Add the tomato paste, garlic, cumin, pimentón, and salt and cook until very fragrant, about 30 seconds.

Add the tomatoes and their juice, the black beans, and the corn. Cook, stirring, until the corn is just tender, about 3 minutes. Turn off the heat, stir in the nutritional yeast (if using), and season the mixture to taste with additional salt if needed.

Finish the pie

Pour the topping mixture evenly over the black bean mixture. Bake until the cornmeal topping is firm to the touch, browned on top, and a toothpick inserted in the center of the cornmeal mixture tests clean, 25 to 30 minutes.

Make the sauce and serve

While the pie bakes, place the vegan mayonnaise, lime juice, and salt in a small bowl and whisk until smooth.

Serve the pie warm and drizzle each serving with some of the sauce.

A THOUGHT

ON SINGING + WHY RECIPES MATTER

Do you know the worst way to get a soft-spoken person to speak louder? By telling them to speak louder. I know this because I am not a loud person. I'm not shy, I'm just soft-spoken. I don't mind talking in front of big groups of people if there's a microphone. I don't mind talking to people I don't know. I just have a hard time raising the volume of my voice. So even if I'm calm, confident even, people can't always hear me. After a lot of reflection on this, and therapy, and a little push from my wife, I decided that I'd like to be heard more. So I did something that terrified me. I went to a singing workshop.

It was a couple of years ago right at the end of the year, post–holiday blitz, and right after I had finished a particularly grueling stretch of work. I wasn't quite burnt out, but I was nearly there. I went to the workshop, away from my day-to-day responsibilities, turned off my phone, and I sang my little heart out.

I was in a group of about twenty women. Some had been in singing groups for decades, one was a performer, another was a kindergarten teacher looking to bring back songs for her students. We spent two hours on Friday, five hours on Saturday, and two more on Sunday just singing together. Our teacher would sing us a few lines of a song and we would sing them back to her. We weren't given any papers with words on them. We just had to listen and repeat. Listen and repeat. We sang in rounds, and I learned what rounds even are, and we learned hand gestures to match some of the lyrics. We just went for it. At a certain point I couldn't tell where their voices ended and mine began.

I felt fully and gloriously present. Doing something that scared me, and something I had to pay my complete attention to, meant I wasn't thinking about anything else. Like literally nothing else. Which doesn't even happen to me when I'm sleeping. That December, in a classroom in rural Massachusetts, I learned it wasn't just my voice I was looking for, it was the feeling of being present.

When I got home, buzzing from my weekend, Grace asked me to sing her something. And I realized I couldn't remember a single song. Not a one. She didn't believe me. She said I had to have remembered something. But all that being present, listening so I could repeat the words back to my teacher over and over again, meant that the whole thing was just a blur. A really empowering, fun, and lovely blur, but a blur nonetheless.

And that's when it hit me: recipes matter. You can spend hours with someone in person or even on a screen showing them how you make your favorite meal, even tell them each ingredient as you add it, and they can be completely present for that exchange. And then they can go home to their kitchen and have no idea how to replicate the experience. If only they had a recipe . . .

When I'm not working on recipes for my books, I never cook with them. It feels a little weird for me to say that in a cookbook full of recipes I've written, but in my non-book writing everyday life I cook intuitively and add a little of this, a little of that. When Grace asks me how long something will take in the oven, I reply "until it's done." I trust my instincts, instincts based on so many years of cooking. Just like my singing teacher knew all those words, all those movements, and all the unspoken mechanics that make her singing seem effortless.

So even though I don't always follow recipes, I believe strongly in providing them. In making sure your questions are answered before you might even know you have them. In singing you my favorite songs and giving you the lyrics so they can be yours, too.

And just like our singing teacher encouraged us to riff on our last day together (TERRIFYING!), I'm also cheering for you whenever you might want to try putting the recipe aside and cooking, "singing," whatever feels right. At the end of the day, recipes are suggestions, not prescriptions. They're guidelines. You can trust mine, but I also trust you. Your kitchen and your meals are just that: yours. Sing!

CARIBBEAN PELAU WITH KIDNEY BEANS + SPINACH

There's a recipe in my first book, *Small Victories*, for Jennie's Chicken Pelau, the one-pot chicken-and-rice dish that Jennie, my childhood babysitter, made all of the time when I was growing up. A staple of Jennie's native Saint Vincent, pelau is one of Jennie's standby comfort foods and, thanks to her, it's become one of mine, too. These days I find myself making it with kidney beans and some spinach instead of the chicken, making it a hearty, vegan, gluten-free pot of food that even the most carnivorous folks can get behind (it's even Jennie-approved). The trick to pelau is to first burn some sugar in oil. It seems against most cooking instincts. You're purposefully burning your food. And yet the finished dish doesn't taste burnt at all, it just tastes layered. Don't flinch at the full tablespoon of salt (remember you're seasoning two cans of beans and a full cup of rice). Serve with cold beer and hot sauce. It's also nice next to a crunchy fresh salad of tomatoes and cucumbers with a little avocado and a lot of fresh lime and salt.

Serve 4 to 6

2 tablespoons canola oil (or other neutral oil such as vegetable)

2 tablespoons granulated sugar

1 large yellow onion, finely diced

1 green bell pepper, stemmed, seeded, and finely diced

3 large carrots, peeled and finely diced

4 garlic cloves, minced

3 tablespoons ketchup

1 tablespoon kosher salt

1 teaspoon ground turmeric

One 13.5-ounce [400 ml] can full-fat coconut milk

1 cup [240 ml] water

1 cup [200 g] long-grain white rice

Two 15-ounce [425 g] cans red kidney beans, rinsed and drained

10 ounces [283 g] fresh baby spinach

Place the canola oil and sugar in a large, heavy pot (like a Dutch oven) over medium-high heat. Cook, stirring, until the mixture is black and smoking, about 4 minutes. You're not looking for caramel. You're looking for burnt. Trust!

Once it burns, turn the heat to medium-low and stir in the onion, bell pepper, and carrots. Cook, stirring, until the vegetables begin to soften, about 10 minutes.

Turn the heat to high and stir in the garlic, ketchup, salt, turmeric, coconut milk, and water. Once the

mixture boils, turn the heat to low and stir in the rice and the drained beans. Cover the pot and cook until the rice is tender, about 25 minutes. Turn off the heat, uncover the pot, add the spinach on top of the pelau (you might need to really pack it in), and then cover the pot. Let the pelau rest for 10 minutes. Uncover the pelau, see that your spinach is wilted, stir everything together, and season one final time with salt. Serve immediately.

STEWY ESCAROLE + WHITE BEANS WITH FENNEL + LEMON

I recently started spending a day each week helping out at farm close to my home run by my friends Sam and Erin (you can "meet" them on page 231). In addition to a hard-earned farmer's tan, I've also gained an increased appreciation for the labor that goes into producing vegetables. And it's helped me appreciate every single leaf, stem, and tuber that I eat. Enter this love letter to escarole, an homage to one of the crops that Sam and Erin lovingly grow. Somewhere between a soup and a stew, this recipe is hearty and comforting. The dried mushrooms give it some umami and depth, and the pop of lemon zest and juice at the end gives it a whole other layer of bright flavor. Serve on its own or with some toasted or grilled bread rubbed with garlic to sop up all of the juices. Or serve over pasta, rice, or polenta.

Serves 4 to 6

3 tablespoons extra-virgin olive oil

1 large fennel bulb, stalks and fronds removed (save for stock!), thinly sliced

Kosher salt

6 garlic cloves, minced

2 teaspoons fennel seeds

1 teaspoon dried red pepper flakes

2 cups [480 ml] vegetable stock (homemade, store-bought, or bouillon paste dissolved in boiling water)

3 dried shiitake mushrooms

Two 15-ounce [425-g] cans white beans, rinsed and drained

1 large head escarole [about 1 pound (453 g)], roughly chopped, washed well

Finely grated zest and juice of 1 small lemon

Place the olive oil in a large, heavy pot (like a Dutch oven) over medium-high heat. Add the fennel and sprinkle with 1 teaspoon salt. Cook, stirring now and then, until the fennel begins to soften, about 10 minutes. Add the garlic, fennel seeds, and red pepper flakes. Cook, stirring, until very fragrant, about 1 minute.

Add the stock and dried shiitakes, turn the heat to high, and bring the mixture to a boil. Turn it to medium and add the drained beans and escarole along with 1 teaspoon salt. Cook the mixture, stirring now and then, until the escarole is completely wilted and very soft, about 10 minutes. Use tongs to remove the mushrooms from the mixture and transfer them to your cutting board. Remove and discard the mushroom stems, then thinly slice the caps and return them to the pot. At this point you can cool the mixture down and refrigerate it for up to a week (or freeze it).

Just before serving, stir in the lemon zest and juice. Season the mixture to taste with extra salt if needed. Serve hot.

MORE-VEGETABLE-THAN-RICE FRIED RICE

Exactly as it sounds, this fried rice stretches a little bit of rice into a big, healthy skillet of food thanks to a ton of vegetables. Kids love this and so do grown-up kids (aka adults). The frozen shelled edamame give you a good boost of protein. If you're not vegan, feel free to scramble a couple of eggs right into the rice. The peanuts add some welcome, salty crunch at the end. Oh, also! If you don't have a chance to defrost your frozen vegetables before using them, just add a few extra minutes to the cooking time or blanch them quickly in a little boiling water (or zap them in the microwave). Feel free to add a big dollop of chili garlic sauce (such as sambal) or other hot sauce if you'd like this to have a kick.

Serves 4

For the stir-fry sauce

1 tablespoon minced ginger

3 garlic cloves, minced

2 tablespoons soy sauce

2 tablespoons ketchup

2 teaspoons rice vinegar

For the rice

4 tablespoons canola oil (or other neutral oil such as vegetable), divided

1 small white or yellow onion, finely chopped

2 large carrots, peeled and finely diced

1 bell pepper (any color you like), stemmed, seeded, and finely diced

Kosher salt

3 cups [240 g] finely shredded green cabbage (about ¼ small cabbage)

2 cups [280 g] cooked brown rice

1 cup [135 g] frozen peas, defrosted

1 cup [135 g] frozen corn kernels, defrosted

1 cup [135 g] frozen shelled edamame, defrosted

½ cup [70 g] roasted, salted peanuts (or almonds), roughly chopped

First, make your stir-fry sauce
Place the ginger, garlic, soy sauce, ketchup, and vinegar in a small bowl. Stir together and reserve.

Next, make the rice
Place 1 tablespoon of the canola oil in a large nonstick skillet over high heat with the onion, carrots, and bell pepper. Season the vegetables with a big pinch of salt and cook, stirring now and then, until beginning to soften and brown in spots, about 5 minutes. Transfer the vegetables to a bowl and reserve them.

Place the skillet back over high heat, add 1 more tablespoon of oil to the pan, and then add the cabbage. Season with a big pinch of salt and cook, stirring now and then, until beginning to soften

and brown in spots, about 5 minutes. Transfer the cabbage to the bowl with the onion mixture.

Place the skillet back over high heat and add the final 2 tablespoons of oil to it. Sprinkle the rice in the pan in an even layer. Let the rice cook, without stirring it, until it smells wonderfully nutty and is slightly crisp on the bottom, about 2 minutes. Add the reserved sautéed vegetables back to the pan along with the peas, corn, and edamame and stir everything well to combine. Pour over the stir-fry sauce and continue to cook, stirring, until everything is hot and a little bit crisp and ready to go, about 1 minute. Season to taste with more salt and/or soy sauce as needed. Sprinkle with the chopped peanuts and serve immediately.

CARROT + CHICKPEA KORMA

Meera Sodha is one of my favorite contemporary cookbook authors (check out *Made in India* and *Fresh India*). She also writes for tons of newspapers and websites and I pretty much always want to cook whatever she describes. She once did a vegan cauliflower korma recipe for *The Guardian* with ground cashews as the base for the sauce. I have played around with cashew-based kormas in my kitchen ever since. My current favorite way to make it is as follows, with carrots and chickpeas. You could also stir in some baby spinach or defrosted frozen spinach at the end if you're looking for something green (peas and/or shredded kale work, too). Serve just on its own, or with warm flatbread for mopping up the sauce, or on top of some cooked rice. The little bit of garam masala, a wonderfully fragrant spice mix, goes a long way here (I get mine online from both Spicewalla and Kalustyan's) and can be used for so many other things (try it tossed with squash, oil, and salt before roasting or in your next lentil soup).

Serves 4

8 medium carrots [about 1½ pounds (680 g)], peeled and cut into 2-inch [5-cm] pieces

3 cups [720 ml] vegetable stock (homemade, store-bought, or bouillon paste dissolved in boiling water)

1 cup [130 g] roasted, unsalted cashews

2 tablespoons extra-virgin olive oil

1 large red onion, thinly sliced into half moons

4 garlic cloves, minced

2 tablespoons minced fresh ginger

½ teaspoon ground turmeric

2 teaspoons garam masala (or ½ teaspoon each ground cumin, coriander, turmeric, and black pepper)

2 tablespoons tomato paste

Kosher salt

One 15-ounce [425 g] can chickpeas, rinsed and drained

Place the carrots and stock in a large, heavy pot (like a Dutch oven) over high heat and bring to a boil. Turn the heat to low and simmer just until the carrots are tender (test by piercing with a paring knife), about 15 minutes. Use a slotted spoon to transfer the carrots to a plate or bowl and reserve them.

Pour the hot stock into a blender with the cashews and let the mixture sit for 10 minutes to let the cashews soften. Blend the mixture until very smooth and hang onto it.

Wipe the pot dry, put it back on the stove over medium-high heat, and add the olive oil to it. Add the onion and cook, stirring now and then, until just beginning to soften, about 5 minutes. Add the garlic, ginger, turmeric, garam masala, and tomato paste. Cook, stirring, until very fragrant, just a minute. Stir in the reserved cashew mixture and season the mixture to taste with salt (don't be shy with the salt; it could be about 2 teaspoons depending on how salty your stock is).

Stir in the chickpeas and the reserved carrots. Turn the heat to high and then just when the mixture begins to bubble, turn the heat to low. Partially cover the pot and simmer the korma, stirring now and then, until the whole mixture is nice and thick, about 10 minutes. Serve hot.

BEST BLACK BEANS
WITH AVOCADO SALAD

When the coronavirus pandemic began, I received a large number of direct messages and emails asking me about my favorite way to cook beans. The recipe that follows, which includes a Puerto Rican–inspired sofrito, is my go-to. The sofrito, a mix of aromatics all ground together, gives the beans so much flavor and dimension without any meat. Most Puerto Rican sofritos include cilantro (or culantro, its botanical cousin), but I skip it here mostly because my wife doesn't enjoy it (that's why I usually call for it on top of dishes—because then it's easy for her to forgo it and I can still enjoy it . . . win-win).

Side note: Illyanna Maisonet, a food writer who documents Puerto Rican foodways, has written extensively about the versatility of sofrito and I highly recommend subscribing to her newsletter for her thoughts on it and just about everything else.

Served with a fresh, acidic salad full of rich avocados and sweet tomatoes, these beans really need nothing else, but I really love serving them with store-bought tortilla or plantain chips for texture, and rice, too.

Serves 4

For the beans

1½ cups [305 g] dried black beans

2 bay leaves

For the sofrito

1 large yellow onion, roughly chopped

1 green bell pepper, stemmed, seeded, and roughly chopped

10 garlic cloves, peeled

2 teaspoons ground cumin

2 teaspoons dried oregano

2 teaspoons pimentón (smoked Spanish paprika)

Kosher salt

¼ cup [60 ml] extra-virgin olive oil

For the salad

2 ripe avocados, peeled, pitted, and thinly sliced

Kosher salt

2 medium ripe tomatoes, cut into thin wedges

½ small red onion, thinly sliced into half moons

2 tablespoons red wine vinegar

2 tablespoons extra-virgin olive oil

First, make the beans
Place the black beans and bay leaves in a large, heavy pot (such as a Dutch oven) and cover with cold water. Bring the mixture to a boil and then immediately turn the heat to low so that it gently simmers. Simmer the beans, stirring them every so often and adding water if needed to keep them covered, until they're very tender, anywhere from 1 hour to 2 or 3 hours (the exact time depends on how old your beans are). This is a great time to work on something else in your kitchen.

Once the beans are tender, reserve 1 cup [120 ml] of their cooking liquid and drain the rest (save for another use such as soup or cooking rice, watering plants, or just discard it). Discard the bay leaves. Wipe the pot dry and hang on to it (you're about to cook the sofrito in it).

Meanwhile, make the sofrito
Place the onion, bell pepper, garlic, cumin, oregano, pimentón, and 1 teaspoon salt in a food processor and pulse until finely chopped (you're

not looking for a smoothie, you're just making life easier for yourself by not chopping everything by hand).

Place the olive oil in the pot you just cooked the beans in over medium heat. Add the mixture from the food processor and cook, stirring now and then, until the vegetables almost melt into each other and the whole mixture is thick and rich, about 12 minutes. Stir in the reserved beans and cup of cooking liquid. Season to taste with additional salt if needed (they will likely need a good amount—don't be shy!).

Next, make the salad
Place the avocado slices in an even layer on a serving platter. Season generously with a big pinch of salt. Top with the sliced tomatoes and red onion and season those with salt. Drizzle with the vinegar and olive oil.

And serve
Serve the black beans warm with the avocado salad. You can eat these next to each other, on top of each other . . . whatever you'd like.

A THOUGHT

A LOVE LETTER TO MY GAS GRILL

I was about twelve when I fired up a gas grill by myself for the first time. It was on the deck of the house I grew up in. I had seen my father do it a number of times and by that age I was already a pretty confident cook. I closed the grill and walked back inside to let the grill heat up. When I came back outside and opened the grill, it was still cold. Realizing it never ignited after I turned the gas on, I pressed the ignition button again. Without thinking through that the gas had been flowing freely for a good fifteen minutes. There was . . . a slight mushroom cloud. When I gasped and instinctively put both my hands on my head, I felt how charred the edges of my hair were. Luckily I wasn't seriously injured, but I sure was spooked.

You might think after that I would never want to touch a gas grill again. But it didn't stop me. And, needless to say, I've never made that mistake ever again. I went right back in as fearlessly as I could and kept on teaching myself how to grill.

Now that I've been (safely) grilling for more than two decades, I can say with some authority that a gas grill, if you have the space for one, is one of the best investments you can make. I use mine multiple times a week. Maybe not as much in the winter, but I do use it year-round. I'll go out with an umbrella if I have to.

I love the convenience of a gas grill. I love being able to go outside and cook dinner and not have to clean up a pan. I can grill a whole bunch of things in one go and Grace and I can repurpose leftovers throughout the week. I can cook for a crowd with ease. I can turn the heat as high as I want and let things get really browned and charred in a way I hate to do inside of my kitchen. Many like to point out that charcoal gets even hotter than gas. Sure, I tell them, but I don't want a whole project. I just want to make dinner.

And despite my early run-in with the mushroom cloud, I love how safe gas grills are. Everything is contained. When I was in fifth grade I was voted safety patrol captain, which I've kind of taken as a lifetime appointment. I get that with charcoal or live fire cooking there's some romance about not having as much control, about dancing with the fire. But with my gas grill, I can just turn it off whenever I'm done. There are no lingering embers or the anxiety that comes with them. And there's no cleaning up ash. It's neat. It's tidy.

I have four pieces of gas-grilling advice. The first is to always have a backup tank of propane waiting somewhere for you. If you run out of gas while you're grilling, you can be sure that you can carry on cooking whatever's on your grates. A backup tank is peace of mind. My second piece of advice is to get a nice big cast-iron pan or griddle and let it heat up on your grill until it's smoking hot. This allows you to cook things that would otherwise fall through or stick to the grates. I'm talking about corn kernels cut off their cobs and cooked with a little bacon. Or shrimp. Or a piece of fish that you've slicked with olive oil and sprinkled with Old Bay. Third is to always have a "landing spot" for whatever you're cooking. This could be a large wooden cutting board or plate on a table next to your grill or a sheet pan waiting on a nearby chair. You need somewhere to put that food. Fourth and final, while your food is grilling, take a deep breath of fresh air. You're outside! Cooking! How great is that?

STEWED CHICKPEAS WITH PEPPERS + ZUCCHINI

A late summer go-to during our volunteering shifts at Angel Food East, this light stew of chickpeas, peppers, and zucchini is the best way I know to use up a ton of summertime produce without a ton of effort. Served with a creamy, lemony sauce and couscous, pasta, rice, or quinoa (or any grain), it's a healthy-and-hearty recipe that is simple to make and infinitely adaptable, too. Swap out the chickpeas for any type of bean. Have extra peppers? Add them! Have a bunch of tomatoes? Chop them up and throw them in. Dice some eggplant, roast it, and fold it in at the end. Add vegetable stock to this and call it soup. Skip the grain or pasta and use the mixture to fill quesadillas. This is flexible cooking, which is my favorite kind of cooking.

Serves 4

For the sauce

1 large handful fresh Italian parsley, finely chopped (a little stem is fine)

3 tablespoons fresh lemon juice

½ cup [120 ml] vegan mayonnaise (or regular mayonnaise if you're not vegan)

½ teaspoon kosher salt

For the stew

3 tablespoons extra-virgin olive oil

1 medium red onion, thinly sliced into half moons

4 garlic cloves, minced

2 bell peppers (red, yellow, and/or orange), stemmed, seeded, and thinly sliced

2 tablespoons tomato paste

2 teaspoons dried oregano

Kosher salt

2 medium zucchini [about ¾ pound (340 g)], ends trimmed, cut into bite-sized pieces

Two 15-ounce [425 g] cans chickpeas, rinsed and drained

¼ cup [60 ml] water

1 tablespoon red wine vinegar

To serve

Cooked couscous, pasta, rice, quinoa, or any other grain

First, make the sauce
Place the parsley, lemon juice, vegan mayonnaise, and salt in a small bowl and stir well to combine. Reserve the mixture.

Next, make the stew
Place the olive oil in a large, heavy pot (like a Dutch oven) over medium heat. Once it's warm, add the onion, garlic, bell peppers, tomato paste, oregano, and a large pinch of salt. Cook, stirring now and then, until the vegetables begin to soften, about 5 minutes.

Stir in the zucchini, chickpeas, water, and another large pinch of salt. Turn the heat to high and when that little bit of water begins to boil, turn the heat to medium-low, cover the pot, and cook, uncovering it every so often to stir, until the zucchini is very soft and the mixture is stewy, about 25 minutes. Turn off the heat, stir in the vinegar, and season the mixture to taste with salt.

Serve the stew warm over the couscous (or whatever you're serving it with). Top each serving with a large spoonful of the sauce.

ROASTED CAULIFLOWER +
RED CABBAGE TACOS

ROASTED CAULIFLOWER + RED CABBAGE TACOS

A one-sheet-pan dinner, these tacos combine nutty roasted cauliflower and cabbage with a bright, creamy avocado sauce. If you don't have a food processor to make the sauce, just mash everything together in a bowl with a fork or a potato masher. It won't be as smooth, but it will still be delicious and provide the right balance for the tacos. What's the best way to warm corn tortillas? If you have a gas stove, just warm them directly over the flame, using tongs to flip them. Once they're a little bit charred, wrap them in a kitchen towel and let them sit and steam amongst themselves for a minute before serving. No gas stove? Do the same in a hot cast-iron skillet.

Serves 4

For the filling

1 small cauliflower [about 2 pounds (907 g)], outer leaves and core discarded, cut into small florets

1 pound [453 g] red cabbage, thinly sliced (about ½ small red cabbage or 6 cups sliced)

¼ cup [60 ml] extra-virgin olive oil

1 teaspoon ground cumin

1 teaspoon ground coriander

1 teaspoon kosher salt

For the sauce

1 ripe avocado, peeled, pitted, and roughly chopped

1 large handful fresh cilantro, finely chopped (a little stem is fine)

3 tablespoons fresh lime juice

3 tablespoons vegan mayonnaise (or regular mayonnaise if you're not vegan)

½ teaspoon kosher salt

To serve

12 small corn tortillas, warmed (see recipe introduction for information on how to warm them)

Finely diced white onion, thinly sliced radishes, pickled jalapeños, and/or hot sauce

First, preheat your oven to 400°F [200°C].

Next, make the filling

Place the cauliflower and cabbage on a large sheet pan. Drizzle with the olive oil and sprinkle with the cumin, coriander, and salt. Use your hands to mix everything together and spread it out into an even layer. Roast, stirring every 15 minutes, until the vegetables are softened and browned in spots, about 45 minutes.

Next, make the sauce

Place the avocado, cilantro, lime juice, vegan mayonnaise, and salt in the bowl of a food processor and puree until smooth. Season to taste with more salt if needed.

And serve

Evenly divide the sauce and roasted vegetables among the tortillas (or set out bowls of everything and let everyone build their own tacos). Serve immediately with the toppings.

GARLIC + SESAME NOODLES WITH MUSHROOMS + BROCCOLINI

Andrea Nguyen, one of the best cookbook authors I know, created a great recipe for umami garlic noodles with mustard greens in her book *Vietnamese Food Any Day.* These noodles, full of garlic and greens, are inspired by hers, but they go in a sesame-heavy direction and include a triple shot of the stuff (tahini paste! toasted oil! seeds!). To balance out the savory sesame, garlic, mushroom combination, the noodles get topped with sweet, fresh tomatoes and a handful of cilantro, which makes everything taste awake (if you're not into cilantro, use a couple of thinly sliced scallions, or just skip it). I love eating this just as it's made, when the noodles are hot and the tomatoes are cold, but it can also be served at room temperature, making it great for entertaining, bringing to work or school, or taking to a picnic.

Serves 4

Kosher salt

8 ounces [227 g] dried Chinese wheat noodles (aka lo mein noodles, or substitute ramen noodles, spaghetti, or buckwheat soba)

1 pound [453 g] broccolini, tough stems discarded, cut into bite-sized pieces

6 garlic cloves, minced

¼ cup [60 ml] soy sauce

2 tablespoons light brown sugar

2 tablespoons well-stirred tahini

2 tablespoons toasted sesame oil

1 tablespoon chili garlic sauce (such as sambal)

3 tablespoons canola oil (or other neutral oil such as vegetable)

½ pound [227 g] cremini mushrooms (or button mushrooms), stemmed and thinly sliced

1 tablespoon sesame seeds

2 large handfuls cherry tomatoes, halved

1 large handful fresh cilantro, roughly chopped (a little stem is fine)

Bring a large pot of water to a boil and salt it generously. Add the noodles and set a timer for 2 minutes less than their package instructs. When it goes off, add the broccolini and cook for just a minute (so you're cooking the broccolini for a minute and the noodles a minute less than they're supposed to). Reserve ½ cup [120 ml] of the cooking liquid and then strain the noodles and broccolini in a colander and hang onto them.

Place the reserved cooking liquid in a small bowl with the garlic, soy sauce, brown sugar, tahini, toasted sesame oil, and chili garlic sauce. Stir well to combine and reserve the sauce.

Place the canola oil in a large nonstick skillet over high heat. Add the mushrooms and cook, stirring now and then, until they're softened and browned in spots, about 5 minutes. Add the sesame seeds and cook, stirring, just until the seeds are fragrant, about 1 minute. Add the reserved sauce mixture and the reserved noodles and broccolini. Cook, stirring everything together with 2 large wooden spoons (like you were mixing a salad) until everything is coated with sauce, about 2 minutes. Season the noodles to taste with salt.

Transfer the noodles to a serving platter. Top with the tomatoes and cilantro. Serve immediately.

SHiiTAKE + PUMPKIN BIRYANi

Ma Kauthar, a home cook on Kenya's Lamu Island, shared a recipe for her chicken biryani in Hawa Hassan's *In Bibi's Kitchen*, a cookbook I got to work on that's all about grandmothers from eight African countries that touch the Indian Ocean. Her biryani, layered with so many different ingredients, inspired this one and its mix of spices and vegetables and the orderly method of combining them. A lot of preparation goes into each layer, but the reward is so memorable.

A few things to keep in mind: to crush the cardamom pods, just press on them with the bottom of a heavy pot or the flat side of your chef's knife. You just want them to crack so their seeds, and thereby their flavor, really emerge. If you don't have cardamom pods, they're widely available online (check out Burlap & Barrel, Diaspora Co., Spicewalla, or Kalustyan's; use extra to make homemade chai). Rinse the rice by placing it in a sieve and running it under a tap while mixing it with your hand so the water rinses every grain, or place it in a bowl of water, agitate it, drain it, and repeat until the water is clear. This rinsing step is important because it gets rid of excess starch, which will help keep the rice grains separate and not clumped together (I do this whenever I make long-grain rice that I want to be fluffy and dry, as I do here, but not when I am cooking rice in something soupy like jambalaya, page 31, or when I am cooking short-grain rice and am looking for a slightly sticky texture). Oh, and if your pot is wider in diameter than 9 inches [23 cm], just do the layering in two parts rather than three.

Serves 4

For the rice

4 cups [1 liter] water

4 green cardamom pods, crushed

4 whole cloves

Kosher salt

1 cup [200 g] white basmati rice, rinsed well (see recipe introduction)

For the mushrooms

3 tablespoons canola oil (or other neutral oil such as vegetable)

¾ pound [340 g] shiitake mushrooms, stems discarded, roughly chopped

For the pumpkin gravy

2 tablespoons canola oil (or other neutral oil such as vegetable)

1 large red onion, thinly sliced into half moons

1 tablespoon minced fresh ginger

4 garlic cloves, minced

2 teaspoons ground cumin

2 teaspoons ground turmeric

1 teaspoon ground cinnamon

2 tablespoons tomato paste

One 14.5-ounce [411 g] can diced tomatoes with their juice

One 15-ounce [425 g] can pumpkin puree (not pumpkin pie filling!)

For the finishing the layers

½ cup [70 g] roasted almonds, roughly chopped

½ cup [100 g] dried apricots, roughly chopped

1 large handful fresh cilantro, roughly chopped (a little stem is fine)

First, preheat your oven to 400°F [200°C].

Make the rice

Put a medium ovenproof pot over high heat and add the water, crushed cardamom pods, cloves, and 1 tablespoon salt. Bring to a boil, add the rice, partially cover, and cook until the rice is barely tender, about 10 minutes. Drain the rice in a fine-mesh sieve and reserve it. You can either pick out and discard the spices now, or leave them mixed in, let them flavor the whole dish, and just let your guests know to look out for them when you serve the biryani in a little while. All good either way.

Then, make the mushrooms

Return the now-empty pot over high heat and add the 3 tablespoons of the canola oil. Once the oil is hot, add the mushrooms. Cook, stirring now and then, until beginning to soften and brown in spots, about 8 minutes. Season the mushrooms to taste with salt, transfer them to a plate, and reserve them.

Make the pumpkin gravy

Add the remaining 2 tablespoons of canola oil to the pot along with the onion. Cook, stirring now and then, until just softened, about 5 minutes. Add the ginger, garlic, cumin, turmeric, cinnamon, and tomato paste and cook, stirring, until very fragrant, about 30 seconds. Stir in 1 teaspoon salt, the tomatoes with their juice, and the pumpkin puree. Turn the heat to high and cook until the mixture starts to bubble, as if it were a hot porridge or polenta, then immediately turn the heat to low. Gently simmer just until the sauce gets to more fully develop its flavor, about 10 minutes. Turn off the heat and season the sauce to taste with salt. Transfer the sauce to a bowl. No need to wash the pot.

Last, layer and bake

Transfer a third of the rice to the now-empty pot and top it with a third of the mushrooms, a third of the sauce, a third of the almonds, and a third of the apricots. Repeat the process two more times. Cover the pot, place in the oven, and bake until the rice is cooked through and incredibly fragrant, about 30 minutes.

Remove the biryani from the oven and let it sit, covered, for 10 minutes before uncovering. Top with the cilantro. Serve immediately straight from the pot.

4

ELEVEN CHICKEN RECIPES

WINKY, HOPE + GRACE, 2020
(EVERYONE ♡S CHICKEN CUTLETS!)

ALMOND CHICKEN CUTLETS FOR GRACE

When Grace was first diagnosed with type 1 diabetes, she switched to eating a low-carbohydrate diet so that it was easier to learn all the ins and outs of insulin (to make something complicated overly simple, the more carbohydrates you eat, the more insulin you need to take). It was a scary time for us and as we figured out our new normal, I dove into the kitchen, where I always feel a sense of control even if there's no such thing. I started making low-carb versions of Grace's favorite foods, including chicken cutlets.

We've eased up on the restrictions in our house as the years have passed, but these chicken cutlets have stuck. They're actually just so much easier to make than regular fried ones because you don't have to dredge them and you just bake them (much easier than cleaning a splattered stove). You could swap the chicken breasts for chicken tenders, boneless and skinless chicken thighs, big squares of tofu, or fish fillets. Grace likes to stir together a little bit of barbecue sauce with mayonnaise for serving, which I highly recommend. Other ideas include an elegant squeeze of lemon, a ramekin of Parmesan + Peppercorn Dressing (page 146), or just some good old ketchup.

Serves 4

2 tablespoons mayonnaise

2 tablespoons Dijon mustard

¼ cup [27 g] almond flour

1 tablespoon Old Bay Seasoning (or 1 teaspoon each kosher salt, sweet paprika, and garlic powder)

Four 6-ounce [170 g] boneless, skinless chicken breasts

Cooking spray (my preference is olive oil spray, but use whatever you have)

Preheat your oven to 400°F [200° C]. Line a sheet pan with parchment paper and set it aside.

Place the mayonnaise and mustard in a small bowl and stir well to combine.

Place the almond flour and Old Bay in a small bowl and stir well to combine.

Place the chicken breasts on the sheet pan. Evenly divide the mustard mixture among them and use a spoon, pastry brush, or your fingertips to spread the mixture to coat the surface of each chicken breast. Sprinkle a quarter of the almond mixture evenly over each chicken breast. Spray each one with a thin coat of cooking spray.

Bake the chicken breasts until they're browned, firm to the touch, and register at least 165°F [74°C] on a digital thermometer, about 30 minutes. Cut each chicken breast into thick slices and serve immediately.

A THOUGHT

ON THE WORTHINESS OF OUR BODIES

MY MOM + ME, 1988

In having the privilege to write a book that's all about healthy comfort food, I think it's important to be honest about my feelings about my own body while suggesting all sorts of things you can cook to feed yours. It's important, also, to acknowledge that these feelings are evolving.

For as long as I've always loved food, I've also been as conflicted about consuming it. A few years ago, it really hit me how much time and energy I had spent feeling bad about myself, especially about my body. And that made me feel really sad. So I decided to start untangling the knot. I knew it wouldn't magically untie itself just because I wanted it to. I had to get some help.

What did that help look like? So many things. I tackled hard stuff in therapy, I changed who I follow on social media to learn more about people who had broken free from diet culture, I researched what diet culture actually is, I read books and listened to podcasts about intuitive eating and shame and vulnerability, and I started to speak more openly to my closest friends about their relationships to their bodies. I began to talk honestly with my mother about how much I absorbed from watching her not treat her own body with kindness. I stopped (*I'm trying to stop*) asking my wife to reassure me that my body is okay. I hid my scale in a closet, and then, one day when I finally felt ready, I threw it away.

I've had a handful of breakthrough feelings throughout this ongoing shift. One was, after many gentle suggestions, Grace finally got me to watch *The Matrix* and it's given me the most helpful framework to think about diet culture. Now when I think about it, a culture that prioritizes thinness and urges us to keep comparing ourselves to each other so that we're left feeling really isolated, I simply think *Oh, that's not actually real.*

Another major breakthrough was when I realized I had limited my range of feelings to just two options. It hit me one day like a splash of cold water in the face. I had only ever felt two things in my life: happy or fat. I remember feeling like a light switch had turned on in a dark room. *Oh, that's what's been going on in here.*

For so long, whenever I felt fat, or what I deemed fat, it was almost always a way to describe anything other than happy. Not only had I equated "fat" with "anything other than happy," I had set up a tidy, miserable binary for all of my feelings to fit into.

How did I get to this restricted emotional place? Through the same roads so many people I know have also traveled. I inherited body image and weight issues, I internalized the bullying I experienced when I was younger when I was told repeatedly that I was fat and understood it to be an insult. What else? I unflinchingly accepted the idea that thin is ideal, and I put myself in close proximity with people who didn't challenge any of this. I listened to doctors tell me I was overweight according to charts whose problematic origins I didn't ask about, and I didn't push for more information when they told me my blood work was great, but I should still lose some weight. I didn't ask them why. I put my head down.

So how did I begin to dig my way out of this dark hole? I started to believe my wife when she said there was a version of my life that didn't revolve around feeling bad about my body. I started to change who I was talking with and looking at and listening to. I followed the money and started questioning all of the programs and people who were telling me my life could be so much better *if only you did this thing I am selling you*. I realized they stay wealthy if I stay desperate. I dug into the things that made me feel all the things other than happy. I started to question how I measure happiness. I learned how many different, and more loving, barometers exist. I made an effort to stop using the word "should" (I even got a tattoo of it, crossed out, on my arm). I stopped equating "fat" with "bad." I watched the "Fat Babe Pool Party" episode of *Shrill* on television so many times (written by Samantha Irby, one of my favorite writers, and developed by Lindy West) and went from crying to smiling.

I became an observer of myself. I bought an "EMOTIONS" poster, the kind you see in little kids' classrooms that list tons of emotions and depict a child making a face that represents each. I made myself go look at the poster to figure out what I was actually feeling in the moment and which emotions they were tied to.

It turns out that the more I understand my range of feelings, and actually feel them, the more I get to know myself. I'm a more imperfect, silly, and complicated person than I ever knew. I screw up a lot. I bump into so many things all of the time, literally and figuratively. I rewrote this very essay at least a dozen times. And that's okay.

Just like cooking, I work on feeling my feelings on a daily basis. Sometimes it's really challenging. Each time I willingly step outside of the framework I grew so accustomed to, I encounter things like pain, anger, sadness, embarrassment, and fear. All of those things that fall under "anything other than happy." But I'm also encountering more love, joy, confidence, and satisfaction than I ever knew was possible. I am learning what it feels like to not merely accept my body, but to understand that there's nothing wrong with it. To love it. To know that no matter how much space it takes up in the world, it's worthy and I'm grateful to live in it.

It should not feel revolutionary to say, especially in a cookbook that's about healthy cooking, that fat does not equal bad or unlovable. But it's worth saying. There is nothing wrong with being fat. The only thing wrong is thinking that any person, living in any type of body, is less valuable than someone else.

SPINACH + ARTICHOKE DIP CHICKEN BAKE

Inspired by the classic dip, this chicken is a weeknight wonder because it relies on frozen spinach and canned or jarred artichoke hearts (I'm down for anything that doesn't require a ton of prep but delivers big flavor). Serve with rice, potatoes of any kind (including roasted sweet potatoes), noodles, and/or a big salad. If you find it difficult to mix everything together in the skillet before baking, just use a big mixing bowl and then return everything to the skillet.

Serves 4

3 tablespoons extra-virgin olive oil, plus more if needed

1½ pounds [680 g] boneless, skinless chicken breasts or thighs, cut into bite-sized pieces

1 teaspoon kosher salt, divided

½ teaspoon freshly ground black pepper, divided

4 garlic cloves, minced

One 10-ounce [283 g] package frozen leaf spinach, thawed, drained, and squeezed very dry

One 14-ounce [255 g] can or jar artichoke hearts, drained, halved

1 cup [240 g] sour cream

½ cup [70 g] finely grated Parmesan cheese

Preheat your oven to 425°F [220°C].

Place the olive oil in a large oven-safe nonstick skillet over medium-high heat. Add half of the chicken to the pan and season with half of the salt and pepper. Cook, stirring now and then, until browned all over, about 5 minutes. Transfer the chicken to a large bowl and repeat the process, adding another tablespoon or so of oil to the pan, if necessary, with the rest of the chicken.

Return the first batch of chicken to the skillet. Add the garlic, spinach, artichoke hearts, and sour cream and stir well to combine.

Sprinkle evenly with the cheese. Place the skillet in the oven and bake until the cheese is browned, about 20 minutes. Serve hot.

STICKY CHICKEN

During the first few days of being together, Grace and I ended up on a spontaneous road trip that included dinner at a friend-of-a-friend's-mom's house (got that?). She served what she called Sticky Chicken, small pieces of chicken coated with a very glossy glaze. Based on Chinese stir-frying traditions, it's such a flavorful dish that comes together quickly thanks to a host of pantry ingredients. Each time I make it, I'm taken back to those very early, exciting days of our relationship when it felt like a light switch I didn't know about got flipped on, like everything finally made so much sense. While I can't promise all of that with this recipe, I share it with all the joy that comes with the memory. Serve with rice or noodles or steamed bok choy or broccoli or roasted sweet potatoes or stir-fried snap peas . . . the list goes on.

Serves 4

2 tablespoons water

1 teaspoon cornstarch

¼ cup [60 ml] ketchup

3 tablespoons honey

3 tablespoons soy sauce

1 tablespoon chili garlic sauce (such as sambal), or your favorite hot sauce (optional)

4 garlic cloves, minced

2 tablespoons canola oil (or other neutral oil such as vegetable), plus more as needed

1½ pounds [680 g] boneless, skinless chicken breasts or thighs, cut into bite-sized pieces

Kosher salt

Freshly ground black pepper

Place the water and cornstarch in a small bowl and stir well to combine. Stir in the ketchup, honey, soy sauce, chili garlic sauce (if using), and garlic. Reserve the sauce.

Place the canola oil in a large nonstick skillet over high heat. Add half of the chicken to the pan and season generously with salt and pepper (about ½ teaspoon of each) and cook, stirring now and then, until browned all over, about 5 minutes. Transfer the chicken to a plate and repeat the process, adding another tablespoon or so of oil to the pan if necessary, with the rest of the chicken.

Return the first batch of chicken to the skillet along with the reserved sauce. Bring the mixture to a boil, then turn the heat to low and simmer, stirring now and then, until the sauce is thick and coats the chicken, about 5 minutes. Serve immediately.

CHICKEN REUBEN SKILLET

When Grace and I feel like going out on a date, we go down the road to Cherries, our local ice cream and sandwich shop. We sit outside and split a big Reuben sandwich with fries and then we get two small ice creams to take with us on a country drive. It's the small things in life that make a life. Inspired by our date-night order, this one-pan chicken recipe is full of spices reminiscent of corned beef or pastrami, plus tons of sauerkraut, a little mayonnaise and ketchup in the spirit of Russian dressing, and Swiss cheese. If you don't have a coffee grinder, you can grind the spices with a mortar and pestle or in a blender (or put them in a small plastic bag and crush them with the bottom of a small, heavy pot or a rolling pin). If you use a coffee grinder that you typically use for coffee and don't want your coffee to taste like a Reuben, just grind some plain white rice in it after you whiz up your spices (discard the rice or use it in your next pot of congee!). Serve this chicken on its own or on top of baked potatoes. You could also serve it on toasted rye or pumpernickel bread or even use it to fill Kaiser rolls. Maybe throw in a big green salad or just some simple green beans. And don't forget to have ice cream afterward.

Serves 4

1 teaspoon kosher salt

2 teaspoons black peppercorns

2 teaspoons caraway seeds

1 teaspoon coriander seeds

1 teaspoon garlic powder

1 tablespoon light brown sugar

1½ pounds [680 g] boneless, skinless chicken breasts or thighs, cut into bite-sized pieces

3 tablespoons unsalted butter

2 cups [350 g] drained sauerkraut

2 tablespoons mayonnaise

2 tablespoons ketchup

1⅓ cups [145 g] coarsely grated Swiss cheese

Preheat your oven to 425°F [220°C].

Place the salt, peppercorns, caraway seeds, coriander seeds, garlic powder, and brown sugar in an electric coffee grinder or spice grinder and blitz until finely ground. Place the chicken in a large bowl, sprinkle with the ground spice mixture, and use your hands to mix everything together.

Place the butter in a large ovenproof skillet over medium heat. Once it melts and begins to bubble, add the chicken and cook, stirring now and then,

until browned all over, just firm to the touch, and barely cooked through (it will finish cooking in the oven), about 8 minutes.

Turn off the heat and stir in the sauerkraut, mayonnaise, and ketchup. Evenly sprinkle the cheese on top of the mixture and tuck the skillet into the oven. Bake until the cheese is melted and gooey and the chicken is completely cooked through, about 12 minutes. Serve hot.

GREEN CHILE BRAISED CHICKEN THIGHS WITH PINTO BEANS

Almost like a light chili, this is one of those things that's not only okay to make ahead, it's actually better if you do. Just rewarm in a pot over low heat (it also freezes well). It's so simple to make. You just brown the chicken, add a can of beans, a can of tomatoes with chiles, and some spices. You don't even need to peel an onion or mince garlic. You can serve this braise on its own as part of a rice or grain bowl. It's also wonderful as a taco or enchilada filling. You can also tuck the chicken and beans inside of a quesadilla or use as a topping for baked potatoes (regular or sweet). If you have a grill and feel like making this outdoors, just grill the chicken thighs instead of browning them in the pot and then place them in a Dutch oven set directly on your grill and follow the rest of the recipe as written. You'll have a cool kitchen, some extra smoky flavor, and some cowgirl credibility.

Serves 4

2 tablespoons olive oil

1 pound [453 g] boneless, skinless chicken thighs

Kosher salt

One 15.5-ounce [439 g] can pinto beans

One 10-ounce [283 g] can diced tomatoes with green chiles (preferably Ro*Tel Original)

1 teaspoon ground cumin

1 teaspoon red chile powder (ground ancho or chipotle are my favorites, but use whatever you have)

2 tablespoons fresh lime juice or brine from a jar of pickled jalapeños

1 large handful fresh cilantro, finely chopped (optional, but if you use it, a little stem is fine)

Sour cream, for serving (optional)

Place the olive oil in a large, heavy pot (like a Dutch oven) over medium-high heat. Season the chicken thighs generously with salt and add them to the pot, in batches as necessary so they don't crowd the pot, and cook until deeply browned on both sides, about 4 minutes per side. Stir the beans into the pot (no need to drain the can), along with the canned tomatoes and chiles, cumin, chile powder, and a large pinch of salt. If you want the braise to have some extra broth, go ahead and fill the empty tomato can with water and add the water to the pot (skip this water if you prefer it to be more stew-like—there's no wrong answer here, it's just personal preference). Turn the heat to high and bring to a boil, then immediately lower the heat,

cover the pot, and simmer until the chicken is incredibly tender, about 1 hour.

Turn off the heat and use 2 forks or tongs to shred the chicken directly into the pot. Season the mixture to taste with more salt as needed. At this point you can let the mixture cool, store it in an airtight container, and refrigerate for up to a week before serving (or freeze for up to a month and defrost overnight in the refrigerator).

Right before serving, stir in the lime juice (or pickled jalapeño brine) and sprinkle with chopped cilantro (if using). Serve hot with sour cream dolloped on top of each serving (if using).

LOW-AND-SLOW BAKED GREEK CHICKEN + POTATOES

This recipe reminds me that patience is always rewarded. Here, a couple hours of gradual cooking leaves you with the most tender chicken and potatoes and liquid gold in the form of delicious pan juices. First you start with a moderate oven and cover the chicken and potatoes, then you uncover them and expose them to the heat a bit more directly, then you raise the heat and let everything brown. A blitzed-up mixture of Greek yogurt, feta, and dill is the perfect condiment. I don't think you need anything else with this, but a chopped salad of cucumbers, tomatoes, bell peppers, and red onion is nice, or a big platter of roasted or grilled zucchini drizzled with olive oil, red vinegar, and torn fresh mint. You could also add chopped zucchini and/or green beans to the roasting dish during the final half hour of cooking.

Serves 4

1 whole chicken, cut into parts (or 4 bone-in, skin-on chicken breasts or 8 bone-in, skin-on chicken thighs)

2 pounds [907 g] Yukon Gold potatoes, cut into large chunks (each about two bites), peeled or unpeeled (up to you!)

¼ cup [60 ml] extra-virgin olive oil

1 cup [240 ml] chicken stock (homemade, store-bought, or bouillon paste dissolved in boiling water)

1 tablespoon dried oregano

1 tablespoon kosher salt, plus more as needed

2 lemons

1 cup [285 g] plain, full-fat Greek yogurt

½ cup [55 g] crumbled feta cheese

1 small handful fresh dill, roughly chopped

Preheat your oven to 300°F [150°C].

Place the chicken, potatoes, olive oil, chicken stock, oregano, and salt in the largest baking dish you have (or a sheet pan). Cut the lemons in half and squeeze their juice over everything and throw the squeezed halves in with it all, too. Mix everything together with your hands and spread it out in an even layer. Make sure the chicken pieces are skin-side-up.

Cover the dish tightly with aluminum foil and bake until the chicken and potatoes are just barely cooked through, about 45 minutes. Uncover the dish and bake until the chicken and potatoes are cooked through but still quite pale, another 45 minutes. Turn the heat up to 400°F [200°C] and roast until the chicken is browned and the potatoes are very tender, a final 30 minutes.

Meanwhile, place the yogurt, feta, and dill in the bowl of a food processor and puree until smooth and whipped, about 1 full minute of the machine running. Season the mixture to taste with salt.

Serve the chicken and potatoes hot with the roasting juices spooned over and the yogurt mixture alongside for dipping.

JALAPEÑO POPPER-STUFFED CHICKEN

One of the most ideal ways to take boring boneless, skinless chicken breasts in a very fun direction, here they get filled with cream cheese and cheddar cheese for richness, fresh jalapeño for kick, and cilantro for brightness. Serve with rice, a stack of warm tortillas, or crusty bread to sop up the delicious pan juices. A pot of black or pinto beans would be nice, too, as would thick slices of avocado and tomatoes seasoned with lime and salt. Iceberg wedges with Jalapeño Vinaigrette (page 152) and chopped cilantro, pictured here, are also a great accompaniment.

Serves 4

Four 6-ounce [170 g each] boneless, skinless chicken breasts

¼ cup [60 g] cream cheese

½ cup [60 g] coarsely grated sharp cheddar cheese

1 fresh jalapeño, stemmed, seeded, and minced

3 tablespoons minced fresh cilantro (a little stem is fine)

Kosher salt

2 tablespoons extra-virgin olive oil

½ teaspoon ground cumin

½ teaspoon pimentón (smoked Spanish paprika)

½ cup [120 ml] water

Preheat your oven to 425°F [220°C].

Place one of the chicken breasts in a large resealable plastic bag and use a meat pounder, rubber mallet, or the bottom of a small-but-heavy pot to pound the chicken so it's ¼ inch [½ cm] thick. Repeat the process with the remaining chicken breasts.

Place the cream cheese, cheddar cheese, jalapeño, cilantro, and ½ teaspoon salt in a small bowl and stir well to combine. Evenly divide the mixture among the pounded chicken breasts and use your fingertips or a rubber spatula to spread it to cover, as if you were buttering toast. Starting with one of the narrower ends of each chicken breast, roll each one up as if it were a miniature yoga mat. Secure each chicken breast with a toothpick or two. Place each chicken breast in a baking dish (or

an ovenproof skillet), toothpicks down (seam sides down).

Place another ½ teaspoon salt in a small bowl with the olive oil, cumin, and pimentón and stir well to combine. Evenly divide the mixture among the chicken breasts and use your fingertips or a pastry brush to coat the exterior of each chicken breast. Pour the water around (not on top of) the chicken breasts.

Roast the chicken breasts until they're nicely browned, firm to the touch, and register at least 165°F [74°C] on a digital thermometer, about 30 minutes. Let the chicken breasts rest for at least 10 minutes before removing the toothpicks. Slice the chicken breasts and serve hot with any extra juices from the baking dish poured on top.

ROAST CHICKEN WITH ONION GRAVY

Add this chicken to the list of recipes inspired by our volunteer work at Angel Food East. To make it, you cut up a chicken, season it, and roast it in a skillet on a bed of sliced onions and chicken stock. After the chicken is cooked, you set the skillet on the stove, reduce the cooking juices just a little bit, and then stir in mustard and sour cream to make a rich onion gravy without any flour, roux, or anything else that usually causes gravy anxiety. Serve this chicken with mashed or crushed potatoes (they're a good place to put more sour cream) and steamed green beans. Or with cornbread and cooked greens. Or with noodles and peas. Or with rice and buttered broccoli. Or with warm rolls and roasted squash. You get the idea . . .

Serves 4

1 large (or 2 small) yellow onion, thinly sliced into half moons

2 cups [480 ml] chicken stock (homemade, store-bought, or bouillon paste dissolved in boiling water)

Kosher salt

Freshly ground black pepper

1 whole chicken, cut into 8 parts (or 4 bone-in, skin-on chicken breasts or 8 bone-in, skin-on chicken thighs), patted dry with a paper towel

3 tablespoons unsalted butter, cut into 8 thin slices

2 tablespoons Dijon mustard

½ cup [113 g] sour cream

Preheat your oven to 400°F [200°C].

Place the sliced onion and chicken stock in a large, heavy, ovenproof skillet (I use a cast-iron one for this). Season the mixture with a large pinch of salt and a few grinds of black pepper.

Place the chicken pieces, skin-side-up, on top of the onion mixture and season them generously with salt and pepper. Place a butter slice on top of each piece of chicken and roast until the chicken is browned, firm to the touch, and registers at least 165°F [74°C] on a digital thermometer, about 45 minutes.

Use tongs to transfer the chicken pieces to a serving platter and cover them with foil to keep them warm.

Place the skillet with the onions on the stove and bring to a boil over high heat. Let the mixture boil for 5 minutes to thicken slightly, then turn the heat to low. Whisk in the mustard and sour cream and season the gravy to taste with salt and pepper. Pour the mixture over the chicken pieces. Serve immediately.

KHAO MAN GAI

I've always admired people who do one thing and do it so well. One of the best examples of this is Nong Poonsukwattana from Nong's Khao Man Gai in Portland, Oregon. She started off with a small food cart making one thing, traditional Thai khao man gai, and eventually grew to operate multiple brick-and-mortars all revolving around this wonderful dish of poached chicken, rice, broth, sliced cucumber, cilantro, and a ginger-garlic-soy sauce.

It's seemingly simple, but the care and attention Nong pays is extraordinary. She renders the extra fat from the chicken with lots of aromatics and uses it to cook the rice. She poaches the chicken with more aromatics and uses that fortified stock in the rice, too; it's also the broth you get with your meal. The sauce is so good that she started bottling it for eager customers. The whole thing is, in my mind and in the minds of so many others, a perfect meal. The feeling of eating there is so joyful and I appreciate that she pays as much attention to her staff as she does her cooking: Nong's employees all receive full medical and dental insurance. Being that Nong's is one of Grace's favorite places in the world and we live far away from it, I set off to make a simple version we eat at home often. It's not Nong's, but it's close and it's comforting. I hope you enjoy it as much as we do.

Serves 4

For the chicken

4 cups [1 liter] water

One 3-inch [7.5-cm] piece fresh ginger, roughly chopped (no need to peel)

4 garlic cloves, crushed

2 teaspoons kosher salt

1½ pounds [680 g] boneless, skinless chicken breasts or thighs

For the sauce

2 tablespoons boiling water

1 tablespoon white miso paste (or Thai fermented soybean paste, which is more traditional)

1 tablespoon honey

2 garlic cloves, minced

2 tablespoons minced fresh ginger

3 tablespoons soy sauce

2 tablespoons rice vinegar

To serve

Cooked white rice, sliced cucumber, and fresh cilantro leaves

First, prepare the chicken
Place the water, ginger, garlic, and salt in a medium saucepan set over high heat. Bring to a boil, then turn the heat to low. Add the chicken, cover, and gently simmer until the chicken is firm to the touch and cooked through (cut into a piece to test it if you'd like), about 30 minutes. Turn off the heat and let the chicken sit in the warm broth while you prepare the sauce.

Next, prepare the sauce
Whisk all of the sauce ingredients together in a small bowl.

To serve
Use tongs to transfer the chicken to a cutting board and cut into thick slices. Strain the broth through a sieve into a bowl or pitcher. Divide it among 4 small bowls. Divide the chicken among 4 large plates, top with the sauce, and put a bowl of broth on each plate. Add a scoop of rice, a pile of cucumber, and some fresh cilantro to each plate. Serve immediately.

STEWED CHICKEN WITH SOUR CREAM + CHIVE DUMPLINGS

Comfort in a bowl, this stewed chicken is inspired by my favorite potato chip flavor (and if that doesn't make you want to try this, I'm not sure what will). After preparing this recipe, you might find some leftover sour cream and chives in your refrigerator. Use them to top your next baked potato or cheese omelet. Or for a quick dip, finely chop the chives, mix them with the sour cream, and season with salt and lemon.

Serves 4, generously

For the chicken

2 tablespoons unsalted butter

1½ pounds [680 g] boneless, skinless chicken breasts

Kosher salt

Freshly ground black pepper

2 cups [480 ml] chicken stock (homemade, store-bought, or bouillon paste dissolved in boiling water)

4 large carrots, peeled and cut into bite-sized pieces (on the diagonal if you'd like to be fancy!)

5 ounces [141 g] fresh baby spinach

For the dumplings

1 cup [125 g] all-purpose flour

2 teaspoons baking powder

2 teaspoons onion powder

1 teaspoon kosher salt

½ cup [113 g] sour cream

¼ cup [60 ml] water

3 tablespoons minced fresh chives

First, make the chicken
Melt the butter in a Dutch oven (or another heavy, wide pot) over medium-high heat. Generously season the chicken breasts with salt and pepper on both sides and cook until browned on both sides, about 5 minutes per side.

Add the chicken stock and carrots to the pot and bring the mixture to a boil. Turn the heat to low, cover the pot, and simmer until the chicken and carrots are tender, about 30 minutes. Transfer the chicken breasts to a large plate or bowl and use a couple of forks to shred the meat (use one to hold the chicken down and the other to pull the pieces). Return the chicken to the pot along with the spinach. Stir well to combine and to wilt the spinach. Keep warm over low heat.

Next, prepare the dumplings
Place the flour, baking powder, onion powder, and salt in a large bowl and whisk well to combine. Stir in the sour cream, water, and chives.

Finish the dish
Evenly dollop the dumpling batter on top of the chicken mixture in large spoonfuls (each about 2 tablespoons or so). Turn the heat to high and bring the mixture to a boil, then turn the heat to low, cover the pot, and cook until the dumplings are just cooked through, about 15 minutes.

Turn off the heat and let the pot sit, undisturbed, for 10 minutes. This allows the dumplings to finish their cooking in the gentle residual heat. Serve immediately.

HONEYMOON CHICKEN

During our honeymoon, Grace and I shared a bowl of sopa Azteca, also known as tortilla soup, the Mexican chicken soup made with chiles and topped with fried tortillas. I don't know if it was the setting or what was in the bowl, but to this day, I can't eat the soup without feeling like we're still on our honeymoon (I kind of always feel that way, to be honest). This chicken gets roasted on a bed of torn corn tortillas and aromatics that later get blitzed into a sauce that tastes so much like sopa Azteca that in our home, I've come to think of it as Honeymoon Chicken. Serve with rice and beans or warm tortillas or creamy grits (like the Cheesy Ranch Grits on page 140).

Serves 4

1 whole chicken, cut into parts (or 4 bone-in, skin-on chicken breasts or 8 bone-in, skin-on chicken thighs)

2 tablespoons extra-virgin olive oil

Kosher salt

2 teaspoons red chile powder (ground ancho or chipotle are my favorites, but use whatever you have)

1 teaspoon ground cumin

½ teaspoon ground cinnamon

1 large yellow onion, roughly chopped

1 large tomato, cored and roughly chopped

4 garlic cloves, crushed

Three 6-inch [15-cm] corn tortillas, torn into bite-sized pieces

½ cup [120 ml] chicken stock (homemade, store-bought, or water or beer work)

1 or 2 canned chipotle peppers, plus 1 tablespoon of their accompanying adobo sauce

1 large handful fresh cilantro, finely chopped (a little stem is fine)

Preheat your oven to 400°F [200°C].

Place the chicken in a large bowl, drizzle with the olive oil, and sprinkle with 1 teaspoon salt, and the chile powder, cumin, and cinnamon. Use your hands to rub the oil and seasonings all over the chicken.

Place the onion, tomato, garlic, and tortilla pieces in a large ovenproof skillet. Mix them together with your hands and spread the mixture out in an even layer. Place the seasoned chicken pieces, skin-side-up, on top of the vegetable mixture.

Roast until the chicken is browned, firm to the touch, and registers at least 165°F [74°C] on a digital thermometer, 45 to 50 minutes.

Transfer the chicken to a serving dish and tent with aluminum foil to keep it warm.

Transfer the onions, tomato, garlic, tortilla pieces, and any cooking juices from the skillet into a blender along with the chicken stock. Add one of the canned chipotle peppers and the tablespoon of adobo sauce. Blend until smooth, and if you'd like it spicier, add the second pepper (easier to add one than take it out!). Season the sauce to taste with salt.

Pour the sauce over the chicken. Sprinkle with the cilantro and serve.

5

ELEVEN GREAT SOUPS
+ STEWS

TRIPLE CARROT SOUP

With all the flavor you could possibly get from a carrot, this soup is wonderfully intense thanks to a triple dose of carrot: stock made of carrot peels, sautéed carrots, and carrot juice. I like to top this with a dollop of sour cream and/or a spoonful of Lemon, Mint + Almond Relish (page 154). It also goes wonderfully with grilled cheese sandwiches as an alternative to tomato soup. Know that it freezes well, so go ahead and make a double batch and your future self will thank you.

Serves 6

1 large yellow onion

1 pound [453 g] carrots (about 6 medium carrots)

Kosher salt

3 cups [720 ml] chicken or vegetable stock (homemade, store-bought, or bouillon paste dissolved in boiling water)

2 tablespoons extra-virgin olive oil

3 cups [720 ml] carrot juice

For serving

Coarsely ground black pepper, Lemon, Mint + Almond Relish (page 154), and/or sour cream (all optional)

Peel the onion and carrots and place the ends, roots, and peels in a large pot with 1 teaspoon salt and the stock. Set the pot over high heat, bring the mixture to a boil, turn the heat to low, and simmer while you get the rest of the soup going.

Roughly chop the onions and carrots. Place the olive oil in a large, heavy pot (like a Dutch oven) over medium-high heat. Add the vegetables and season with 1 teaspoon salt. Cook, stirring now and then, until the vegetables begin to soften, about 10 minutes. Add the carrot juice to the vegetables and then ladle the stock through a handheld sieve directly into the pot (or strain it through a colander into a bowl and then add to the soup; either way, discard the onion and carrot peels).

Turn the heat to high and bring the soup to a boil. Turn it to low and simmer until the carrots are

extremely tender (test with a paring knife), about 20 minutes.

Puree the soup with an immersion blender, or with a regular blender. If using the latter, transfer only enough soup at a time to the blender to fill the container no more than one-third full, place the lid on the blender, and put a kitchen towel on top of the blender in the event any hot liquid or steam wants to escape. Start on low speed and slowly work your way up to high to completely puree the soup. Safety always!

However you puree the soup, season it to taste with salt as needed. Serve hot, topped, if you'd like, with pepper, Lemon, Mint + Almond Relish, and/or sour cream.

JODY'S FRENCH LENTIL + KALE STEW

Working with Jody Williams on *Buvette: The Pleasure of Good Food*, her cookbook named for her restaurants of the same name, was one of the most enjoyable professional experiences I've ever had. Jody, who also runs the famed Via Carota in New York with her wife, Rita Sodi, is a funny, warm person who has the best taste in everything from food to hand soap to glassware. And her stewed French lentils with kale, which as of this writing continue to be on the Buvette menu, are a great example of what makes her such a great cook. They're simple and not encumbered by too many ingredients or techniques. They're about patience and the willingness to let something cook low and slow and letting it all just surrender. They're warming and comforting.

Here's my ever-so-slightly-adjusted version (the biggest difference being that I add way more garlic and serve it with ricotta, which you can skip if you're vegan). If you make these in advance, be sure to wait until you reheat the lentils to add the vinegar and nutmeg so they hit the mixture just before serving. Also note that if you want a little bit of flavorful meat in the mix, start the recipe by browning some sausage (reduce the oil to a single tablespoon) and then go from there.

Serves 4

3 tablespoons extra-virgin olive oil

1 small red onion, finely diced

8 garlic cloves, minced

1 pound [453 g] kale (preferably lacinato or dinosaur kale), rinsed, tough stems discarded, coarsely chopped (2 standard bunches)

1 cup [200 g] French lentils (also known as Le Puy lentils)

6 cups [1.5 liters] chicken or vegetable stock (homemade, store-bought, or bouillon paste dissolved in boiling water)

2 teaspoons kosher salt

½ teaspoon freshly ground black pepper

2 teaspoons sherry vinegar

¼ teaspoon freshly ground nutmeg

Whole milk ricotta, for serving

Place the olive oil in a large, heavy pot (like a Dutch oven) over medium heat. Add the onion, garlic, and kale and cook, stirring now and then, until the vegetables begin to soften, about 5 minutes. Add the lentils, stock, salt, and pepper. Turn the heat to high, bring to a boil, then turn to low.

Partially cover the pot and let the mixture simmer gently, stirring every so often, until the lentils are softened, a solid 1½ hours, possibly up to 2 or 2½ hours depending on the age of your lentils. If the mixture threatens to dry out as it cooks, add a splash of water. You want this to be a stew, not a soup, but at the same time you don't want it to be a dry dish. Note that the liquid will be quite dark and murky looking from the lentils. This is just fine!

Just before serving, stir in the vinegar and nutmeg. Season to taste with more salt if needed. Serve hot or warm in bowls with a big spoonful of ricotta on top of each serving.

MUSHROOM + BARLEY SOUP FOR DAD

While it might not win a beauty contest, classic mushroom and barley soup is my dad's favorite. I love it, too, especially on a cold day. Roasting the mushrooms helps to concentrate their flavor, it means you don't have to sauté them in batches to get them brown, and it also lets you cook them at the same time as your barley. I love when something that makes a recipe easier and more efficient also makes it taste better. Note that leftover soup will thicken as it cools. Thin it out to your liking with more stock or water when you reheat it. As my grandma likes to say, it's the soup that never goes away!

Serves 8

1 pound [453 g] cremini (or button) mushrooms, stemmed and finely chopped (about 4 cups)

3 tablespoons extra-virgin olive oil, plus 2 extra tablespoons

Kosher salt

1 large yellow onion, finely diced

2 large carrots, peeled and finely diced

4 large celery stalks, finely diced

4 garlic cloves, minced

10 cups [2.3 liters] beef, chicken, or vegetable stock (homemade, store-bought, or bouillon paste dissolved in boiling water)

1 cup [195 g] pearl barley

6 dried shiitake mushrooms, rinsed

Preheat your oven to 400°F [200°C].

Place the cremini mushrooms on a sheet pan in an even layer. Drizzle with the 3 tablespoons olive oil and sprinkle with ½ teaspoon salt. Use your hands to toss everything together. Roast the mushrooms, stirring occasionally, until they are tender and most of their liquid has evaporated, about 30 minutes. Reserve the mushrooms.

Meanwhile, place the remaining 2 tablespoons olive oil in a large, heavy pot (like a Dutch oven) over medium heat. Add the onion, carrots, and celery. Sprinkle with a large pinch of salt and cook, stirring now and then, until the vegetables begin to soften, about 10 minutes. Stir in the garlic and cook until just fragrant, about 30 seconds. Add the stock, barley, and dried mushrooms. Turn the heat to high and bring the mixture to a boil, then immediately turn the heat to low. Simmer the soup until the barley is just tender, about 30 minutes.

Use tongs to retrieve the dried mushrooms from the pot and place them on your cutting board. Remove and discard the stems. Finely chop the caps and return them to the soup along with the roasted mushrooms. Allow everything to simmer until the barley goes from just tender to very tender, about 20 more minutes. Season the soup to taste with salt. Serve hot.

SMOKED TROUT CHOWDER

Rich without being too thick, this chowder harnesses the flavor of smoked fish to make it taste like you put in a lot of time and effort without actually having to (and no one needs to know . . .). You could use any type of smoked fish in place of the trout or use half a pound of shucked clams, oysters, mussels, or fresh crab, or a pound of fresh shrimp or cubes of fresh cod. Serve with oyster crackers.

Serves 8

2 tablespoons unsalted butter

1 large yellow onion, finely diced

2 large celery stalks, finely diced

1 tablespoon Old Bay Seasoning (or 1 teaspoon each kosher salt, sweet paprika, and garlic powder)

1 pound [453 g] baking potatoes, peeled and cut into ½-inch [1-cm] cubes

One 8-ounce [240 ml] bottle clam juice

2 cups [480 ml] water

1½ cups [360 ml] half-and-half

One 8-ounce [227 g] package ready-to-eat smoked trout fillets, broken into small pieces (discard any skin and/or bones)

Kosher salt

Place the butter in a medium, heavy pot over medium heat. Once it melts, add the onion, celery, and Old Bay and cook, stirring now and then, until the vegetables are just softened, about 10 minutes. Add the potatoes, clam juice, water, and half-and-half and turn the heat to high. The moment it starts to boil, turn the heat to low and stir in the trout. Simmer the chowder until the potatoes are tender, about 15 minutes. Season to taste with salt. Serve hot.

GOLDEN CHICKEN BROTH WITH REAL EGG NOODLES

I never got to meet my maternal grandmother, but I feel a real tether to her in my kitchen. During Passover, the Jewish holiday when foods with any type of leavening are customarily avoided, she used to make egg "noodles" out of just eggs. She would make a stack of incredibly thin omelets, almost like egg crepes, roll the stack up like a huge cigar, and then cut them across into ribbons. When we were in the early days of Grace's type 1 diabetes diagnosis a few years ago, eager for comforting dishes that were low in carbohydrates, I immediately thought about my mom's stories about how wonderful those egg noodles were. They've since become a favorite in our house. While we both love them in a simple bowl of golden chicken broth, they're great in so many different types of broth.

For a pho-inspired broth, you can char some onion, garlic, and ginger in a broiler and then simmer them with stock and lots of cilantro stems, a whole star anise, and a cinnamon stick; then strain all of that after about an hour, and season the broth with fish sauce. For a Mexican-inspired broth, try simmering your favorite dried chile peppers, garlic, and cilantro stems in stock. And on and on. Whatever broth you do, you can add some greens at the end of cooking and also poach some chicken breasts or thighs in the broth for added heft, but I particularly love the simplicity of broth and delicate egg noodles. If you want to make this ahead, store the broth and egg noodles separately and then combine them just before serving to best preserve their texture.

Serves 4

For the broth

9 cups [2 liters] water

1 large yellow onion, roughly chopped (no need to peel)

1 pound [453 g] chicken backs, bones, and/or wings

1 teaspoon freshly ground black pepper

Kosher salt

For the egg noodles

4 large eggs

½ teaspoon salt

Cooking spray
(my preference is olive oil spray, but use whatever you have)

First, make the broth

Place the water, onion, chicken parts, pepper, and 1 tablespoon salt in a large pot over high heat. Don't fear the large quantity of salt (remember you're seasoning all of that water).

Bring the mixture to a boil, skim off and discard any foam that rises to the top, and then turn the heat to low. Simmer the broth gently so that it just barely bubbles and cook until the chicken pieces totally fall apart and the broth is incredibly fragrant, about 2 hours. Ladle the broth through a fine-mesh sieve into a clean pot (or, if you don't have another large pot, ladle it into a bowl, clean the pot you started with, and return the broth to the pot). Discard the contents of the sieve (everything in it will have given all it can by this point, but by all means feel free to pick the chicken meat and snack on it; it won't have much flavor, but there's something very satisfying about standing next to a steaming pot and doing this).

(continued)

Season the broth to taste with additional salt if needed. Keep the broth warm over low heat.

Then, make the egg noodles
Place the eggs in a large bowl with the ½ teaspoon salt and whisk very well.

Set a medium nonstick skillet over medium-high heat and spray the surface with cooking spray. Add enough of the beaten eggs to just coat the bottom of the pan and swirl the pan to coat the surface with the egg (pour any excess back into the bowl). Let the thin omelet cook just until it's cooked through (no need to flip as it's so thin) and then transfer it to a plate. Repeat the process until you've used up all of the beaten eggs, stacking the omelets as you go. Regulate the heat and spray the skillet with cooking spray as needed in between omelets (you might not need to spray between each one depending on the nonstickness of your skillet). You will likely end up with 4 or 5 thin omelets (but it really depends on the size of your pan).

Roll your stack of omelets together and then cut them crosswise into thin ribbons.

Serve
Divide the noodles among 4 large bowls and ladle the broth over them. Serve immediately.

ROASTED CAULIFLOWER SOUP WITH TURMERIC CROUTONS

Yasmin Khan is the cookbook author behind two of my favorite cookbooks, *The Saffron Tales: Recipes from the Persian Kitchen* and *Zaitoun: Recipes and Stories from the Palestinian Kitchen*. I got to interview her for my podcast and we sat at her sister's kitchen table in Brooklyn and talked about making a career transition, the importance of rest, the way food can be an entry point to conversation, and why we have to hold onto hope. After we spoke, she offered me a big bowl of roasted cauliflower soup. It was both comforting and bolstering, just like talking to her.

This soup, which is totally vegan if you use vegetable stock, is inspired by hers. Instead of adding ground turmeric to the soup, as Yasmin does, I used it to flavor the hot oil that coats the croutons to make them extra flavorful. One quick logistic note: if your soup feels a bit thick when you puree it and you'd like it thinner, just add a bit of hot water or additional stock. Some heads of cauliflower are bigger than others, so the amount of stock is more of a ballpark than a prescription. It's your soup and your call! I trust you.

Serves 4

For the soup
1 large cauliflower [about 2½ pounds (1 kg)], outer leaves and core discarded, cut into florets

1 large yellow onion, roughly chopped

3 tablespoons extra-virgin olive oil

2 teaspoons ground coriander

Kosher salt

4 cups [1 liter] hot chicken or vegetable stock (homemade, store-bought, or bouillon paste dissolved in boiling water)

For the croutons
3 tablespoons extra-virgin olive oil

1 teaspoon ground turmeric

⅓ pound [160 g] sourdough bread, torn into bite-sized cubes (about 4 cups)

½ teaspoon kosher salt

First, make the soup
Preheat your oven to 425°F [220°C].

Place the cauliflower and onion on a sheet pan and drizzle with the olive oil. Sprinkle with the coriander and 1 teaspoon salt. Spread everything into an even layer. Roast until the vegetables are softened and browned in spots, about 45 minutes.

Transfer the contents of the sheet pan to a blender with the stock (work in batches if necessary depending on the size of your blender). Carefully puree until extremely smooth (let the blender run for at least a minute once everything has collapsed). If your soup is too thick for your liking, feel free to add a little bit of boiling water or more stock until it's the consistency you like. Season the soup to taste with salt.

Transfer the soup to a pot and keep it warm over low heat while you make the croutons.

Make the croutons
Place the olive oil in a large nonstick pan over medium-high heat. Stir in the turmeric and then immediately add the bread cubes. Give them a toss

and then sprinkle with the salt. Cook, stirring, until the bread absorbs the oil and begins to crisp, about 4 minutes. Transfer the croutons to a plate and let them cool down for at least 5 minutes before serving (they will crisp a bit as they cool).

To serve, ladle the warm soup into bowls, top with the croutons, and enjoy.

ROASTED ONION SOUP

There's a recipe for Parmesan soup in my first cookbook, *Small Victories*, that remains one of my favorite lessons in exhausting all the possible flavor you can from every ingredient you use. Taking a note from my own book (!), this onion soup's broth is made of onion peels and Parmesan rinds that bubble away in stock. While that happens, you slice and then roast the onions whose peels are simmering. By roasting them, you absolve yourself of the responsibility of standing over the stove to caramelize them. The oven does all the work. Once those come out of the oven and mix with the broth, then you melt cheese on bread for croutons for each serving of soup. Dreamy!

One year I made a big batch of this and had a container left over in the refrigerator right before Thanksgiving. Instead of eating the soup, I added it to celery I had softened in a lot of butter, toasted bread cubes, and a few eggs and baked it off on a sheet pan for the most amazing French onion soup stuffing. I just think you should know that this is an option!

Serves 6

4 large yellow onions

10 cups [2.3 liters] beef, chicken, or vegetable stock (homemade, store-bought, or bouillon paste dissolved in boiling water)

One 3-inch [7.5-cm] piece Parmesan cheese rind, plus ¼ cup [28 g] coarsely grated Parmesan cheese

4 tablespoons extra-virgin olive oil, divided

Kosher salt

6 thick slices sourdough bread

1 garlic clove

1 cup [110 g] coarsely grated Swiss cheese (such as Gruyère)

Preheat your oven to 425°F [220°C].

Peel the onions and place the roots and peels in a large pot with the stock and Parmesan rind. Set the pot over high heat, bring the mixture to a boil, turn the heat to low, and simmer while you get the rest of the soup going.

Thinly slice the onions and divide them between two sheet pans. Drizzle 2 tablespoons olive oil over each sheet pan and sprinkle each with ½ teaspoon salt. Use your hands to toss everything together. Roast the onions, stirring occasionally, until they are tender and well browned, about 40 minutes. Reserve the onions and leave the oven on.

Strain the onion broth into a clean pot (or into a bowl, and then return the stock to the pot, and discard the contents of the strainer). Add the roasted onions to the broth and place it over low heat. Season the soup to taste with salt as needed.

Place the bread slices on one of the sheet pans you cooked the onions on. Roast the bread, turning the pieces halfway through, until slightly dry on both sides, about 2 minutes per side. Rub one side of each piece of bread with the garlic clove. Place the grated Parmesan and Swiss cheese in a small bowl and stir to combine. Evenly divide the cheese among the garlic-rubbed toasts and spread to cover. Roast until the cheese melts and is browned in spots, about 8 minutes. Cut each piece of cheesy toast into bite-sized pieces.

Ladle the soup among 6 bowls and top each with the cheesy croutons. Serve immediately.

OLD-SCHOOL BORSCHT

Borscht is a many-splendored thing. I've had my mother's favorite version, which is cold borscht ladled over a hot boiled potato; I've had hot vegan borscht loaded with vegetables and no meat in sight; and I've had hot borscht so full of tender meat that it was almost like Texas chili. This borscht, with a little bit of beef that's browned and simmered with aromatics and a tiny bit of ground allspice (a magical ingredient), then combined with lots of chopped root vegetables, is my favorite. It's a reminder that a small amount of beef can be stretched into a huge pot of food, and also a reminder about the power of time to turn humble ingredients into something pretty special. This borscht is hearty and warming, substantial and beautiful, too. The little splash of vinegar at the end lifts everything up. If you make the soup ahead, add the vinegar just before serving to make sure you get its bright, almost briny effect. And don't forget the sour cream and dill for serving. They're essential.

Serves 6

3 tablespoons extra-virgin olive oil

1 pound [453 g] lean beef stew meat, cut into 1-inch [2.5-cm] pieces, patted dry with a paper towel

Kosher salt

½ teaspoon freshly ground black pepper

1 large yellow onion, finely diced

4 garlic cloves, minced

3 tablespoons tomato paste

½ teaspoon ground allspice

6 cups [1.5 liters] water

3 large carrots, peeled and diced

1 pound [453 g] red beets, peeled and diced (about 4 medium beets)

1 large baking potato [about ¾ pound (340 g)], peeled and diced

3 cups [240 g] finely shredded green cabbage (about ¼ small cabbage)

3 tablespoons red wine vinegar

Sour cream and finely chopped fresh dill, for serving

Place the olive oil in a large, heavy pot (like a Dutch oven) over medium heat. Add the beef, season generously with salt, and sprinkle with the pepper. Cooking, stirring now and then, until it's browned all over, about 10 minutes. Add the onion, garlic, tomato paste, and allspice and cook, stirring, until very fragrant, just a minute. Add the water and use a wooden spoon to scrape up any stuck-on pieces from the bottom of the pot. Bring the mixture to a boil and then immediately turn the heat to low, partially cover the pot (to let steam escape), and simmer until the beef is on its way to tender, about 1½ hours.

Stir in the carrots, beets, potato, and cabbage (don't worry if it seems like there's not a ton of liquid in the soup; the vegetables will release a lot of liquid as they cook). Stir in 2 large pinches of salt. Simmer the borscht, partially covered and stirring every so often, until the beef and vegetables are very tender, about another 1½ hours.

Stir in the vinegar and season the borscht to taste with salt. Serve hot with plenty of sour cream and dill on top of each serving.

CREAMY ROASTED TOMATO + ORZO SOUP

One very freezing winter day I had time to spare before meeting a friend in Brooklyn, so I ducked into a Connecticut Muffin (a Brooklyn-based chain of cafés) to warm up. I got a cup of their soup of the day, tomato orzo. It was so good and so comforting and made me feel warm to the bone. It's now one of my favorite soups to make at home. You just roast canned tomatoes, onions, and garlic, and then blend them with stock and half-and-half and simmer it all with some orzo. To make a vegan version, use vegetable stock and your favorite non-dairy milk (and skip the cheese on top). If you make the soup ahead of time, you can either make the whole thing ahead and reheat it and the orzo will get even mushier and the soup will be thicker, which is sort of cozy; or you can make the soup up until the point of adding the orzo, then reheat just before serving and cook the orzo then. Your soup, your choice.

Serves 4

One 28-ounce [794 g] can whole peeled tomatoes with their juice

1 large yellow onion, roughly chopped

3 garlic cloves, minced

3 tablespoons extra-virgin olive oil

1 teaspoon kosher salt, plus more as needed

3 cups [720 ml] chicken or vegetable stock (homemade, store-bought, or bouillon paste dissolved in boiling water)

1 cup [240 ml] half-and-half

¾ cup [165 g] orzo pasta

Grated Parmesan or pecorino cheese, for serving

Preheat your oven to 400°F [200°C].

Place the tomatoes (with their juice) in a large baking dish with the onions, garlic, olive oil, and salt. Use your hands to mix everything together (no need to break up the tomatoes as you'll blend them in a little while). Roast until the liquid in the dish is mostly evaporated and the onions are tender, about 40 minutes.

Transfer the contents of the baking dish to a blender and puree until smooth.

Transfer the pureed mixture to a large soup pot with the stock and half-and-half. Set the pot over high heat and bring to a boil. Turn the heat to low, stir in the orzo, and cook, stirring now and then, until the orzo is cooked through, about 10 minutes.

Season the soup to taste with salt (it might take about a teaspoon depending on how salty your stock was). Serve hot with grated cheese on top.

MY MOTHER-IN-LAW'S BRUNSWICK STEW

When Grace and I drive to Virginia to visit her folks, my mother-in-law, Elaine, almost always makes a pot of her Brunswick stew to have for dinner when we arrive. A mix of stewed chicken, tomatoes, lima beans, and corn, I've come to look forward to it so much. It's the perfect thing to make ahead since it only gets better if it sits for a day or two in your fridge, plus it's a total one-pot meal since it has so many great vegetables in it.

Like many venerated dishes, there are as many versions of the stew out there as there are Southern cooks, and its origins are blurry (both Brunswick, Virginia, and Brunswick, Georgia, claim to be its birth-place). Some cooks use pork, many older recipes call for squirrel, many include potatoes, and quite a few use barbecue sauce or leftover chopped barbecued meat. When I asked Elaine how she makes hers, she referred me to *Tidewater on the Half Shell: Fine Virginia Recipes*, a cookbook by the Junior League of Norfolk–Virginia Beach. Spiral-bound with a pale peach cover, the book is priceless. The recipe that follows is a riff on that one and uses a rotisserie chicken from the store because life is short and it's nice to take a shortcut sometimes, especially when it brings you exactly where you'd like to go.

Serves 6

1 rotisserie chicken, skin discarded, meat shredded, bones reserved

4 cups [1 liter] water

1 tablespoon extra-virgin olive oil

¼ pound [113 g] bacon (about 4 slices), finely chopped (if you'd like to skip this, just use 2 extra tablespoons of oil)

1 large yellow onion, finely diced

Kosher salt

One 28-ounce [794 g] can diced tomatoes with their juice

One 10-ounce [283 g] package frozen lima beans

Kernels from 3 ears fresh corn [or a 16-ounce [453 g] package frozen corn kernels]

1 teaspoon freshly ground black pepper

2 tablespoons unsalted butter, melted

2 tablespoons all-purpose flour

Place the chicken bones in a medium pot over high heat. Add the water, bring to a boil, turn the heat to low, and simmer while you get the rest of the stew going.

Place the olive oil and bacon in a large, heavy pot (like a Dutch oven) over medium-low heat. Cook, stirring now and then, until all of the fat is rendered and the bacon is crisp, about 4 minutes. Use a slotted spoon to transfer the bacon to a paper towel-lined plate and reserve it (leave the fat in the pot).

Stir the onion into the hot fat and turn the heat to medium. Sprinkle with 1 teaspoon salt and cook, stirring now and then, until the onion begins to soften, about 8 minutes.

Add the shredded chicken meat to the onions along with the tomatoes and their juice. Ladle the chicken stock through a handheld sieve directly into the pot (or strain it through a colander into a bowl and then add to the stew; either way, discard the chicken bones).

Turn the heat to high, bring the stew to a boil, then turn it to low and allow it to simmer until the tomatoes begin to break down, about 10 minutes. Season the mixture to taste with salt.

Add the lima beans, corn, and black pepper and simmer just until the lima beans and corn are tender, about 10 more minutes.

Meanwhile, stir together butter and flour in a small bowl. Stir the mixture into the stew. Simmer until everything is thickened and all the parts come together to make an irresistible sum, a final 20 minutes. Season to taste with salt. Serve hot with the reserved bacon sprinkled on top.

GRACE + HER PARENTS, 1984

ITALIAN SAUSAGE, FARRO + TOMATO STEW

Somewhere between a grain side dish and a hearty minestrone soup, this stew is just the thing when you want a bowl of something that feels like a warm hug. It's also one of the best things I can think of to bring to a friend or family member who needs a little extra support, whether they just welcomed a child or had to say goodbye to someone. The stew can sit in the fridge for a week, or in the freezer comfortably for a month or two. Warm over low heat and eat as is or with a scoop of ricotta (HIGHLY RECOMMEND) or sprinkle with any other cheese (Parmesan, cheddar, feta, whatever). You know what else would be great? A fried or poached egg on top. You could use hot Italian sausage if you prefer more of a kick.

Serves 6

3 tablespoons extra-virgin olive oil

1 pound [453 g] sweet Italian sausage (pork or turkey), casings discarded

2 large yellow onions, finely chopped

2 large carrots, peeled and finely diced

4 garlic cloves, minced

Kosher salt

3 tablespoons tomato paste

One 28-ounce [794 g] can diced tomatoes

1 cup [180 g] farro

½ pound [227 g] kale (preferably lacinato or dinosaur kale), rinsed, tough stems discarded, coarsely chopped (1 standard bunch)

Finely chopped fresh Italian parsley, for serving (optional, but if you use it, a little stem is fine)

Place the olive oil in large, heavy pot (such as a Dutch oven) over medium-high heat. Use your hands to break the sausage into small pieces directly into the pot. Cook, stirring now and then, until browned and crisp, about 8 minutes.

Add the onions and carrots to the pot, turn the heat to medium, and cook, stirring now and then, until the vegetables begin to soften, about 8 minutes. Add the garlic, 1 teaspoon salt, and the tomato paste and cook, stirring, until very fragrant and most of the moisture from the tomato paste has evaporated, about 1 minute.

Add the diced tomatoes with their juice. Fill the tomato can with water and add it to the pot. Turn the heat to high and bring the mixture to a boil. While it's coming to a boil, scrape the bottom of the pot with a wooden spoon to dislodge any stuck-on pieces (flavor!). Once it boils, turn the heat to low and stir in the farro and kale.

Partially cover the stew so that steam can escape and simmer it, stirring every so often, until the kale and farro are tender, 30 to 35 minutes. Season the stew to taste with salt. Serve hot with parsley on top (if you'd like, no biggie if not).

6

ELEVEN GO-TO SIDES

MATCHSTICK CARROT SALAD

I make this any time I need something fresh and crunchy, and it's particularly awesome because you can make it up to three days ahead (just store in a container in your refrigerator) and it will still feel fresh and crunchy. It's a versatile side dish that can be served with everything from a bowl of steamy beans to roast chicken to fried eggs doused with yogurt. Also note that if you don't feel like cutting the carrots into matchsticks, you can coarsely grate them, or slice them into thin rounds (and then you can call it Copper Penny Salad like I once saw in a church cookbook).

Serves 4

2 tablespoons extra-virgin olive oil

2 tablespoons fresh lemon juice (or lime juice or whatever vinegar you have)

1 teaspoon honey

½ teaspoon kosher salt

A pinch of coarse dried red pepper flakes (optional)

¾ pound [340 g] carrots, peeled (4 or 5 medium carrots)

1 large handful fresh Italian parsley, finely chopped (a little stem is just fine)

In a medium bowl, whisk together the olive oil, lemon juice, honey, salt, and red pepper flakes (if using). Thinly slice the carrots on the diagonal into coins and then stack the coins up in manageable piles and cut crosswise into matchsticks. I find this relaxing and meditative—I hope you do, too. Add the carrots to the bowl along with the parsley and mix well. Serve immediately or store in a container in the refrigerator for up to 3 days and serve cold or at room temperature.

JUNE'S CORN SALAD

June's Corn Salad

My mom doesn't cook often, but she is an expert prepared-food-store shopper. When I was growing up she frequented a store called June & Ho, named for its owners, and would always get a container of their corn salad because my dad adored it. This corn salad, an ode to June's, can sit well in the refrigerator for up to a few days and goes well with anything from grilled chicken to steak, sautéed shrimp, or a big pot of black beans. It also makes an excellent taco topper and a great component of a grain bowl. Note that breaking the corn cobs in half makes getting the kernels off the cobs much easier. Also note if you don't like cilantro, you can substitute parsley for it, or skip it altogether.

Serves 4

3 tablespoons extra-virgin olive oil

3 tablespoons fresh lime juice

½ teaspoon kosher salt

½ small red onion, finely diced (about ¼ cup)

Kernels from 3 ears fresh corn [or a 16-ounce (453 g) package frozen corn kernels]

1 medium cucumber, ends trimmed, finely diced

1 large handful fresh cilantro, finely chopped (optional, but if you use it, a little stem is fine)

Place the olive oil, lime juice, and salt in a large bowl and whisk well to combine. Stir in the onion and allow the mixture to sit while you prepare the corn.

Bring a small pot of water to a boil and add the corn kernels. Cook until bright yellow and tender, 1 to 3 minutes depending on how old the corn is. Drain the corn in a colander and immediately stir it into the onion mixture. Let the mixture sit for at least 5 minutes just so it's not so hot. Stir in the cucumber and cilantro. Season the salad to taste with more salt if needed. Serve at room temperature.

ASPARAGUS + SNAP PEAS WITH PEANUTS + BASIL

On your table in about ten minutes, this quick side dish delivers a ton of flavor with little effort thanks to pantry staples like toasted sesame oil, fish sauce, and peanuts. You can blanch the vegetables up to a few days in advance (store wrapped in a paper towel in a container in your refrigerator) and then toss with the dressing, peanuts, and basil right before serving. Serve with rice and a fried egg for an easy meal, or as part of a larger spread with other vegetables and maybe a big grilled fish or a whole chicken roasted and brushed with soy sauce and butter. If asparagus and snap peas aren't in season (or you don't like them), try this with blanched green beans, carrots, broccoli, and/or peas.

Serves 4

Kosher salt

1 pound [453 g] asparagus (about 1 large bunch), tough ends discarded, cut into bite-sized pieces

½ pound [227 g] snap peas (about 3 cups), stemmed and stringed

1 tablespoon soy sauce

2 teaspoons rice vinegar

2 teaspoons toasted sesame oil

1 teaspoon fish sauce

1 teaspoon honey

3 tablespoons dry-roasted, salted peanuts, roughly chopped

1 large handful fresh basil leaves (about 12 large leaves), roughly torn

Bring a large pot of water to a boil and salt it generously. Add the asparagus and snap peas and cook until bright green and barely tender, about 1 minute. Drain the vegetables in a colander, rinse with cool water to stop them from cooking, and then place them on a clean kitchen towel to absorb any extra moisture.

Place the soy sauce, rice vinegar, sesame oil, fish sauce, and honey in a large bowl and whisk well to combine. Add the vegetables, peanuts, and basil and toss well to combine. Season to taste with salt. Serve immediately.

ON COOKING + ANXIETY

When I've been at my most anxious, I've felt like life is one long grocery list that includes something I need that I can't find anywhere. Anxiety is widespread and while it's comforting to know I'm not the only one who can feel its muscular pull, I wish it was something we could all be free from. And yet.

Sometimes I think I was born with a list of things I was worried about (epigenetic inheritance is real!) and sometimes I think I do a very good job of finding new things to worry about all by myself. In addition to therapy, sleep, physical activity (whether it's walking or exercise or gardening), and talking to my wife and my friends, cooking has also been a majorly calming force in my life. While food has definitely brought up plenty to make me feel anxious about (see "On the Worthiness of Our Bodies" on page 78), making it has been the most consistent tool I have to help me feel grounded.

Food has always helped me walk through doors that feel scary. I didn't attend many parties in high school, so when I first got to college and my new friends invited me to go to parties, I smiled and said yes while I quietly panicked inside. Be comfortable at a party? Hang out with people from school besides at school? I wasn't so sure about that. Being someone who doesn't like to arrive anywhere empty-handed, even a college house party, I quickly learned that I could assuage my social anxiety if I stopped at the corner deli, bought the biggest bag of potato chips I could find, and brought them with me. They gave me an easy way to walk up to people without feeling totally awkward. "Want a potato chip?" felt a lot easier than saying "hello." Sure, it was a shtick, but the chips gave me a way in. I eventually became comfortable at parties and other occasions without a bag of chips, but the chips helped pave that comfort.

The other way I've always gone about making friends is inviting people over for a meal. In fact, when I moved into my freshman dorm, I brought a pot and a toolbox filled with basic kitchen tools so it would be easy to take them in and out of the communal kitchen. Those tools, a wooden spoon and a peeler and tongs and such, made me feel like I had the things I needed to do something I loved to do in a place that felt so unfamiliar. They made me feel secure. I made spaghetti for my floormates and roasted chicken in disposable aluminum pans from the grocery store. It was a way to extend myself to my new community.

When I moved into an apartment off campus, I saved up money to buy my first sturdy Dutch oven. I remember a friend telling me that my pot was "so grown up." It made me feel adult when I wasn't so sure what that was (still don't always know, by the way). Cooking not only calmed me, it also helped me feel like I could make the big world I found myself in feel a little bit smaller.

Anxiety, like many complicated things, has so many edges. When I need to exit a stressful setting, or group of people, cooking also lets me do that. In other words, it's not just a way to connect, it's also a way to disconnect. You can always leave your dining room table to do some dishes or to "get dessert ready" even if it's already ready. The kitchen can be a place to take a breath. It's part of why I love grilling so much. It means I get to be outside while everyone is inside. I'm still part of the party, I'm making the food!, but I get to be a little bit at arm's length. And sometimes, that's exactly where I feel most calm.

When I talk to other people about anxiety, I always like to find out when people feel most themselves, most free of worry. For me, it's when I'm standing in my kitchen by myself cooking because I feel like it, not because I need to. There's music playing. I can hear my wife doing something in the other room. I can see our dogs lazily napping on the bench by the kitchen window. I am chopping vegetables, doing the thing that so many other people are doing at the same time around the world. I am alone, but I am also in solidarity. I am content and present. I know what I'm making and have everything I need to do so. I don't care if it turns out perfectly. It's just dinner. I'm worried about nothing.

POTATO SALAD BY REQUEST

My friend Tanya runs an exercise studio called 30 Minutes of Everything® that's honestly changed my life. It's a nonjudgmental space (there are zero mirrors!) and Tanya focuses completely on our form and strength, not our weight or anything like that. She's taught me about how much your feelings can shift when you shift how you measure your success. I know this is an odd introduction to a potato salad recipe, but this recipe is for Tanya, who enjoyed it one day at our house and said, "This will be in your next book, right?" Here it is, Tanya! Note that the secret to this is dressing the potatoes while they are warm. That lets all the flavor from the vinegar and mustard really find its way into the potatoes. Not only is this potato salad okay to make in advance, it's better if you do since it's best served at room temperature or cold.

Serves 4 to 6

1½ pounds [680 g] baby yellow potatoes (about 30 small potatoes)

Kosher salt

3 tablespoons Dijon mustard

1½ tablespoons apple cider vinegar

½ teaspoon freshly ground black pepper, plus more to taste

1 large celery stalk, finely chopped (about ½ cup)

½ small red onion, finely chopped (about ¼ cup)

3 tablespoons mayonnaise

1 large handful fresh Italian parsley, finely chopped (a little stem is fine)

Place the potatoes and a very large pinch of salt in a saucepan and cover with cold water. Set the saucepan over high heat and bring the water to a boil. Turn the heat to low and simmer until the potatoes are tender (test with a paring knife), about 15 minutes. Drain the potatoes in a colander and let them rest until they're just cool enough to handle but still warm.

While the potatoes are cooking and resting, place the mustard, vinegar, and pepper in a large bowl with 1 teaspoon salt and whisk well to combine. Stir in the celery and onion.

Once the potatoes are cool enough to handle (but still warm! don't forget!), cut them in half and stir them into the mustard mixture. Allow the mixture to cool to room temperature and then stir in the mayonnaise and parsley. Season to taste with salt and pepper. Serve immediately or cover and refrigerate for up to 4 days (season to taste again if serving from cold).

TANYA, 2020

PALM SPRINGS PEARL COUSCOUS + CITRUS SALAD

My parents once went on a trip to Palm Springs and couldn't stop raving about the couscous salad they had at a restaurant called Cheeky's. My dad loved it so much that he ordered a second portion for dessert. They even took a picture of the menu and texted it to me. I set out to re-create it in my own kitchen so I could make it for them, and it's been a frequent player on our table ever since. It's great at room temperature, which makes it an ideal thing for company since I can prepare it ahead of time. It also complements so many dishes, from other vegetable salads for a cold lunch to grilled fish for an easy dinner. The key to this recipe is toasting the pearl couscous before adding the water. It adds a whole other dimension.

Serves 4

3 tablespoons extra-virgin olive oil

1 cup [155 g] pearl couscous

1¼ cups [300 ml] water

Kosher salt

2 tablespoons red wine vinegar

3 tablespoons minced red onion

2 navel oranges (preferably Cara Cara oranges if you can find them), peeled and cut into ¼-inch [½-cm] half moons

½ cup [55 g] crumbled feta cheese

¼ cup [32 g] salted, roasted pistachio kernels, roughly chopped

1 small handful fresh parsley or cilantro, finely chopped (a little stem is just fine)

Place the olive oil in a medium saucepan over medium heat. Add the couscous and cook, stirring, until it browns and smells very nutty, about 2 minutes. Add the water and 1 teaspoon salt. Bring the mixture to a boil, turn the heat to low, cover the pot, and simmer until the liquid is absorbed and the couscous is tender, about 10 minutes.

Transfer the warm couscous to a serving bowl and stir in the vinegar and red onion. Let the couscous cool to room temperature and then gently stir in the oranges, feta, pistachios, and parsley. Season the salad to taste with salt. Serve at room temperature.

GRACE'S GREEN BEANS WITH GARLIC + TOMATOES

Grace makes these beans all the time and I love them. She says, "Cook these slowly, don't stir them too much, and butter at the end makes everything better." Trust my wife. If you'd like, sprinkle the cooked beans with crumbled feta just before serving.

Serves 4

2 tablespoons extra-virgin olive oil

1 pound [453 g] green beans, ends trimmed

12 ounces [340 g] cherry tomatoes (1 pint), halved

3 garlic cloves, thinly sliced

½ teaspoon kosher salt

½ teaspoon freshly ground black pepper

1 tablespoon unsalted butter

Place the oil in a large nonstick skillet over medium heat. Once it's warm, add the green beans, tomatoes, garlic, salt, and pepper. Cook, stirring now and then, until the tomatoes are collapsed and the green beans are tender and browned in spots, about 25 minutes. Add the butter and stir just until it melts and coats the vegetables, about 1 minute. Season to taste with salt and serve warm.

HASSELBACK CARROTS WITH
PIMENTÓN + ROASTED LEMON

HASSELBACK CARROTS WITH PIMENTÓN + ROASTED LEMON

These are SO FUN. Inspired by Hasselback potatoes (the sliced and fanned out potatoes that originated at the Hasselbacken restaurant in Stockholm), the key to these carrots is to boil them before roasting them so that they are both soft inside and a little crispy on the outside.

Serves 4

8 medium carrots [about 1½ pounds (680 g)], peeled

2 tablespoons extra-virgin olive oil

1 teaspoon pimentón (smoked Spanish paprika)

Kosher salt

1 lemon, halved

½ cup [120 g] full-fat plain yogurt (regular yogurt, not thick Greek yogurt)

1 garlic clove, minced

1 small handful fresh Italian parsley, cilantro, and/or mint, roughly chopped (a little stem is fine)

3 tablespoons salted, roasted almonds, roughly chopped

Preheat your oven to 400°F [200°C].

Place a large pot of water over high heat. Once it comes to a boil, add the carrots and cook until barely tender, about 10 minutes. Place 2 tablespoons of the cooking water in a small bowl and then drain the carrots and let them hang out until they're cool enough to handle.

Add the olive oil, pimentón, and ½ teaspoon salt to the bowl with the cooking liquid and whisk well to combine. You'll use this mixture in a moment.

Working with one carrot at a time on your cutting board, place a skewer or chopstick on either side of the carrot and slice each crosswise into very thin slices without cutting through the entire carrot (the skewers will help keep you from cutting through the carrots). Place the carrots in a roasting dish, cut sides up. If one or more carrots break into

pieces during this cutting or transferring, don't worry about it. They'll still be great even if they're not whole!

Drizzle the olive oil mixture evenly over the carrots. Place the lemon halves in the roasting dish and roast until everything is browned in spots and the carrots are very tender, about 40 minutes.

Use tongs to squeeze the juice from the lemon halves over the carrots (I like to leave the lemon halves in the dish since they're so beautiful, but feel free to discard them).

Place the yogurt, garlic, and ½ teaspoon salt in a small bowl and whisk well to combine. Dollop the yogurt sauce on top of the roasted carrots and sprinkle with the herbs and almonds. Serve immediately.

SWEET + SPICY MASHED SWEET POTATOES

This mash can be at home next to just about anything. Grilled pork chops, roast chicken, glazed tofu, stir-fried corn and green beans, seared scallops . . . it's friends with everyone. You can make it for a weeknight dinner or a holiday spread. Roasting the sweet potatoes before mashing them, rather than boiling or steaming them, concentrates their flavor. Whipping them in a food processor with salt, a little butter for richness, honey for extra sweetness, and chipotle hot sauce for a smoky kick makes them irresistible. If you don't have a food processor, just mash them by hand with a potato masher. While they won't be silky smooth, they'll still be great. If you'd like to make these in advance, just reheat in a pot over low heat (stir while you heat) or place in a casserole dish in a 350°F [175°C] oven until warm, about 25 minutes (stir a few times while in the oven).

Serves 4 to 6

2 pounds [907 g] sweet potatoes (about 4 medium sweet potatoes)

2 tablespoons unsalted butter

2 tablespoons chipotle hot sauce (such as Cholula, and start with just a little bit at a time if you don't like things too spicy)

2 tablespoons honey

1 teaspoon kosher salt

Preheat your oven to 400°F [200°C].

Line a sheet pan with parchment paper or aluminum foil (this will make cleanup much easier later) and place the sweet potatoes on it. Pierce each sweet potato a couple of times with a paring knife or a fork (this will let steam escape). Bake the sweet potatoes, turning them once or twice while they cook, until very tender (test by squeezing them or check if a paring knife can pierce them easily), about 1 hour.

Let the sweet potatoes sit at room temperature until they're cool enough to handle. Once they've cooled down, peel the sweet potatoes (discard the skins or snack on them—I love them) and transfer the peeled sweet potatoes to a food processor. Add the butter, chipotle hot sauce, honey, and salt. Blitz until very smooth. Season to taste and feel free to add more butter, chipotle hot sauce, honey, and/or salt if you'd like. Serve warm.

BRAISED RED CABBAGE + GREEN APPLES

Sometimes I feel like I am more like a grandfather than a thirty-something woman. I like a cheesy joke, a sturdy sneaker, a nice bowl of soup, a quiet evening, an early morning walk, and, most of all, anything made with cabbage. Cabbage is cheap, versatile, and lasts forever in your refrigerator. It's good raw, roasted, steamed, stir-fried, and especially great braised. This recipe, wonderfully sweet-and-sour thanks to green apples, vinegar, and brown sugar, is foolproof. Serve with roast pork, grilled or roasted sausages, roast chicken, or as part of a grain bowl. I especially love this as a holiday side dish since it can be made in advance and warmed over low heat just before serving. Plus the color is gorgeous!

Serves 4 to 6

3 tablespoons unsalted butter

1 pound [453 g] red cabbage (about ½ medium red cabbage), thinly sliced (about 7 cups)

2 green apples, peeled, cored, and coarsely grated

¼ cup [60 ml] water

¼ cup [60 ml] red wine vinegar

3 tablespoons light brown sugar (or granulated sugar)

1 teaspoon kosher salt, plus more as needed

½ teaspoon freshly ground black pepper

Place the butter in a large, heavy pot (like a Dutch oven) over medium heat. Once it melts, add the cabbage and apples and cook, stirring now and then, until beginning to soften, about 15 minutes. Add the water, vinegar, brown sugar, salt, and pepper. Turn the heat to high and bring the mixture to a boil. Turn it to low, partially cover the pot (allow some steam to escape), and simmer, stirring every so often, until the cabbage is very tender, about 30 minutes. Season to taste one final time with salt (and/or additional vinegar and/or sugar). Serve hot.

WHITE PIZZA-STYLE KALE

There's almost always a bunch of kale in our refrigerator. Most nights I finely chop it, cook a little minced garlic in oil, add the kale and a splash of water and a sprinkle of salt, give it all a good stir, and call it a night. But sometimes after I do that, I dot the top with milky ricotta and grated mozzarella and pop the whole skillet under the broiler so that the cheese melts. Then I shower the whole thing with my favorite pizza condiments: grated Parmesan, dried oregano, garlic powder, and red pepper flakes. Giving kale the white pizza treatment is one of the best ways I know to take the boring out of eating your greens.

Serves 4

2 tablespoons extra-virgin olive oil

2 garlic cloves, minced

1 pound [453 g] kale (preferably lacinato or dinosaur kale), rinsed, tough stems discarded, coarsely chopped (2 standard bunches)

3 tablespoons water

½ teaspoon kosher salt

½ cup [117 g] whole milk ricotta cheese

½ cup [55 g] coarsely grated mozzarella cheese

2 tablespoons finely grated Parmesan cheese

½ teaspoon dried oregano

½ teaspoon garlic powder

½ teaspoon dried red pepper flakes (optional)

Position your oven rack 6 inches [15 cm] from the broiling element and turn the broiler to high.

Place the olive oil in a large ovenproof skillet over medium heat. Add the garlic and cook, stirring, until it begins to sizzle, about 1 minute. Add the kale and water and then sprinkle with the salt. Cook the kale, stirring now and then, until it's softened and the water has evaporated, about 5 minutes.

Turn off the heat. Dollop the ricotta cheese evenly on top of the kale and sprinkle evenly with the mozzarella cheese.

Broil until the cheese is melted and bubbling, about 2 minutes. Keep an eye on the skillet as broilers vary and yours might take a little less, or a little more, time.

Sprinkle the kale with the Parmesan cheese, oregano, garlic powder, and red pepper flakes (if using). Serve immediately, straight from the skillet.

CHEESY RANCH GRITS

From my kitchen to yours, the most comforting side dish I can think of. The name says it all. What's not to love? Grits. Cheese. The taste of ranch dressing. I highly recommend serving these grits right after cooking them so that they stay super creamy and also because they're irresistible and why postpone pleasure? But you can also make them in advance and keep them in the fridge for up to a few days. Rewarm over low heat (add a little extra water or milk to loosen them) or store them in a covered casserole dish in the fridge and then just pop the whole thing in a 350°F [175°C] oven until warm, about half an hour (stir a few times while in the oven).

Serves 4 to 6

2 cups [480 ml] water

2 cups [480 ml] whole milk

2 teaspoons kosher salt, plus more if needed

1 cup [130 g] stone-ground grits

1 cup [110 g] coarsely grated sharp cheddar cheese

3 tablespoons minced fresh chives

1 teaspoon garlic powder

1 teaspoon onion powder

1 teaspoon dried mustard powder

Place the water, milk, and salt in a medium saucepan over high heat and bring the mixture to a boil. While whisking, slowly pour in the grits. Turn the heat to low and simmer the grits so that they ever so gently sputter, stirring often to keep them from sticking, until the grits are very tender, about 40 minutes.

Stir in the cheese, chives, garlic powder, onion powder, and mustard powder. Season the grits to taste with salt. Serve hot.

7

ELEVEN SALAD DRESSINGS,
EASY SAUCES + RELISHES

YOGURT, TAHINI + PARSLEY SAUCE

CHERRY + ALLSPICE SAUCE

JALAPEÑO VINAIGRETTE

ROASTED PEPPER + CORN RELISH

LEMON, MINT + ALMOND RELISH

CREAMY FETA + SCALLION DRESSING

EASY SALSA
VERDE

GO-TO
DRESSING

PARMESAN +
PEPPERCORN
DRESSING

LEMON,
POPPY SEED
+ YOGURT
DRESSING

CREAMY MISO
+CASHEW DRESSING

GO-TO DRESSING

This dressing is SO EASY and requires no cutting or peeling anything—it's just stirring a few pantry items together. It's equal parts tahini, soy sauce, olive oil, and apple cider vinegar (feel free to swap for any type of vinegar or lemon juice). That's it. You don't even need salt since the soy sauce adds enough salinity. You can jazz this up if you want with a minced fresh garlic clove, some chopped herbs, or a big pinch of smoky chile powder—but it doesn't *need* any of those things. Since it's in equal parts, you can make as little or as much as you want. Just cooking a quick meal for yourself? Whisk a spoonful of each ingredient together in the bottom of your salad bowl, then add a handful of greens and whatever else you have, and call it a day. Making dressing for a crowd? Blend everything together by the cupful. Just use equal parts. Also this is great on *everything*. From a simple salad, to a large grain bowl with tons of different elements, to a piece of plain roast chicken that needs a little extra something, this dressing is friends with everybody.

Makes 1 cup [240 ml]

¼ cup [60 ml] well-stirred tahini

¼ cup [60 ml] soy sauce

¼ cup [60 ml] extra-virgin olive oil

¼ cup [60 ml] apple cider vinegar

Place all the ingredients into a small bowl and whisk together. Store in a jar in the refrigerator for up to 2 weeks.

PARMESAN + PEPPERCORN DRESSING

Pour this over chopped romaine for a vegetarian Caesar-esque salad, spoon on thickly sliced tomatoes in the summer, or drizzle on boiled potatoes that you've gently crushed with a fork. So good.

Makes ¾ cup [180 ml]

½ cup [120 g] mayonnaise (you can swap up to half, or even all of this, with plain yogurt)

2 tablespoons fresh lemon juice

2 tablespoons water

¼ cup [27 g] finely grated Parmesan cheese

1 teaspoon freshly and coarsely ground black pepper

½ teaspoon kosher salt

Place all the ingredients in a small bowl and whisk together. Serve immediately or store in a jar in the refrigerator for up to 1 week.

CREAMY FETA + SCALLION DRESSING

One December I found myself at a singing workshop at a yoga retreat center in Massachusetts (you can read a longer version of this story on page 54 if you'd like). Having never been to anything like this, I asked Anna and E, friends of mine who'd been to this same place, if they had any advice. Their words of wisdom? "Get the feta and scallion dressing at the salad bar."

Here's a version you can make at home (singing not required). If you don't have a food processor, you can make this in a blender, but it's better to double or triple the batch so that the liquid fully covers the blade and it blends easily. Or if you want to go analog, you can finely chop the scallions and mash the feta with a fork and then just whisk everything together. It won't be super smooth, but hey, what is in life? Serve this on crunchy lettuce, spoon over cooked vegetables like roasted sweet potatoes or squash , or mix into a pot of cooked grains for an easy side dish (rice, quinoa, orzo...whatever you'd like).

Makes about ¾ cup [180 ml]

6 scallions, ends trimmed, roughly chopped

1 garlic clove, minced

¼ cup [60 g] full-fat plain yogurt (regular yogurt, not thick Greek yogurt)

1 tablespoon red wine vinegar

1 tablespoon water

½ cup [55 g] crumbled feta cheese

½ teaspoon kosher salt

½ teaspoon freshly ground black pepper

Place all the ingredients into a food processor and puree until smooth. Serve immediately or store in a jar in the refrigerator for up to 1 week.

CREAMY MISO + CASHEW DRESSING

This completely vegan dressing, which borders on dip territory, owes all its lusciousness to raw cashews. When blended with water and some seasonings, cashews go from tough little things to the creamiest substance ever (see the vegan Carrot + Chickpea Korma on page 61 for another example of this). Serve with sliced cucumbers or carrots or use to dress crunchy lettuce like romaine or iceberg. It's also wonderful on thick slices of ripe summer tomatoes, almost like a vegan Caesar. And it makes a lovely condiment for a grain bowl. You can also slather this on fish, tofu, or chicken breasts before cooking quickly under your broiler.

Makes 1½ cups [360 ml]

1 cup [140 g] raw, unsalted cashews

½ cup [120 ml] water

2 tablespoons white miso paste

3 tablespoons rice vinegar

2 tablespoons soy sauce

½ teaspoon kosher salt

Place all the ingredients in a blender and blend on high speed until very smooth, a solid minute of blending. Serve immediately or store in a jar in the refrigerator for up to 1 week.

LEMON, POPPY SEED + YOGURT DRESSING

If it's not clear by now, I've got a real soft spot for old-fashioned foods. This poppy seed dressing is a good example. It's a little retro, a little forgotten-but-shouldn't-be, a little sweet, a little savory. It's great on crunchy lettuce and it's also really lovely on fruit. Try it on sliced cantaloupe, halved strawberries, or juicy peach wedges. It also makes a wonderful coleslaw dressing. Just pour it over shredded cabbage and carrots.

Makes 1 generous cup [about 280 ml]

1 cup [240 g] full-fat plain yogurt (regular yogurt, not thick Greek yogurt)

Finely grated zest and juice of 1 large lemon

1 tablespoon Dijon mustard

1 tablespoon honey

1 tablespoon poppy seeds

1 teaspoon kosher salt

Place all the ingredients into a small bowl and whisk together. Store in a jar in the refrigerator for up to 1 week.

EASY SALSA VERDE

One October my best friends came to spend a weekend at our house. We spent a memorable afternoon cooking a huge meal together. After their kids were tucked into bed and my dogs were settled by the fireplace, we sat down to eat. Our normally talkative group fell silent at the table. That's how you know the food is really good! My friends all requested that I include the recipe for the salsa verde I made that evening, which we all spooned over our roast potatoes, salad, mushrooms, and steak. So here it is, my friends. Serve with steak, chicken, fish, or vegetables (anything!), or mix with equal parts mayonnaise or yogurt or sour cream for a creamy dip. Leftovers are great stirred into chicken, tuna, or potato salad or mixed with hot roasted potatoes or squash.

Makes 1 generous cup [about 280 ml]

1 large or 2 small shallots, minced [or ¼ cup minced red onion]

2 tablespoons sherry vinegar (or red wine vinegar or white wine vinegar)

1 teaspoon kosher salt

2 tablespoons Dijon mustard

2 large handfuls fresh Italian parsley, finely chopped (about ½ cup and a little stem is fine)

2 large handfuls fresh cilantro, finely chopped (about ½ cup and a little stem is fine)

½ cup [120 ml] extra-virgin olive oil

Place the shallots, vinegar, and salt in a small bowl and stir well to combine. Let the mixture sit for about 10 minutes just to let the shallots soften a little (this is a good time to get your herbs washed and chopped). Add the remaining ingredients and stir well to combine. Serve either immediately or within a few hours of making to enjoy it at its best (you can refrigerate it for up to a few days, but bring it back to room temperature before serving).

JALAPEÑO VINAIGRETTE

A cross between hot sauce and a salad dressing, this mixture can be used in so many places. Try it on romaine or Bibb lettuce with some sliced avocado and toasted pumpkin seeds. Drizzle on a tomato and peach salad and maybe crumble some crispy bacon on top. Use on your next bowl of rice and beans. Take a heavily salted-and-peppered steak off the grill, slice it, and drench it with this. Mix it with an equal amount of mayonnaise or sour cream and serve it as a dip with everything from chicken fingers to carrot sticks. You can remove the jalapeño seeds if you want it milder (or, alternatively, add more peppers if you want more bite). Don't have a blender? Use a food processor or just finely mince the jalapeño and garlic and whisk everything together.

Makes about 1 cup [240 ml]

1 fresh jalapeño, stem discarded, roughly chopped

4 garlic cloves, roughly chopped

¼ cup [60 ml] fresh lime juice

½ cup [120 ml] extra-virgin olive oil

1 tablespoon granulated sugar

1 teaspoon kosher salt

Place all the ingredients in a blender and blend on high speed until very smooth. Serve immediately or store in a jar in the refrigerator for up to 1 week.

CHERRY + ALLSPICE SAUCE

One day during our volunteer shift at Angel Food East I made some simple pork chops and we had some nice vegetables, but the whole thing felt a little boring. I found a bag of dried cherries in the pantry, threw them in a pot with some red wine vinegar, ground allspice, and water, and let the whole thing simmer for a little while. I pureed some of the mixture and added it back to the pot to thicken the lot without adding an extra ingredient. The sauce was a hit. It made the pork chops more special and it required so little effort. I made it soon after for Thanksgiving in lieu of cranberry sauce and, again, it was a hit. In fact, it's good with just about any roasted or grilled meat (chicken, pork, lamb, or turkey breast are all great). It's also lovely spooned on top of grilled bread spread with soft goat cheese or swiped on your next sandwich along with some mayonnaise. Or serve it with the Swedish Turkey Meatballs (page 10). It even makes for a very sophisticated ice cream topping and is a wonderful thing to stir into your oatmeal. It's such a versatile thing to have on hand and keeps well in the refrigerator for at least two weeks. If you don't have a blender or food processor, just skip the pureeing part and either enjoy as is, or let the sauce reduce a little longer until it's nice and thick.

Makes about 2 cups [280 ml]

2 cups [280 g] sweetened dried cherries (if unsweetened, add ¼ cup [50 g] granulated sugar)

1 cup [240 ml] water

¼ cup [60 ml] red wine vinegar, or to taste

¼ teaspoon ground allspice

½ teaspoon kosher salt, or to taste

Place all the ingredients into a small saucepan over high heat. Bring to a boil, turn the heat to low, and simmer until the cherries are soft, about 5 minutes.

Turn off the heat and let the mixture cool to room temperature. Transfer the mixture to a blender or food processor and pulse to just puree a little of the mixture. You're not looking for it to be super smooth, just slightly pureed so that it sort of thickens itself. You could also use an immersion blender, but be mindful not to blend the entire mixture, just roughly half of it.

Let the sauce cool to room temperature and then season to taste with additional salt or vinegar as needed.

Serve immediately or store in a jar in the refrigerator for up to 2 weeks. Serve at room temperature.

YOGURT, TAHINI + PARSLEY SAUCE

Yotam Ottolenghi, he of so many wonderful cookbooks, has a recipe for a green tahini sauce with lots of parsley and garlic that I love, and I almost always end up serving it next to a bowl of yogurt and encourage everyone around my table to use both on whatever we're eating. This recipe does the combining for you. It works on everything from a chopped salad made of chickpeas and tomatoes and cucumbers and feta, to a bowl of cooked quinoa with rotisserie chicken shredded on top and some roasted broccoli. Try it on roasted zucchini or grilled eggplant. If you don't have a blender, use a food processor. If you don't have one of those, just finely chop the parsley, mince the garlic, and whisk everything together.

Makes 1½ cups [360 ml]

1 cup [240 g] full-fat plain yogurt (regular yogurt, not thick Greek yogurt)

3 tablespoons well-stirred tahini

2 tablespoons fresh lemon juice

2 large handfuls fresh Italian parsley, roughly chopped (about ½ cup and a little stem is fine)

2 garlic cloves, roughly chopped

1 teaspoon kosher salt

Place all the ingredients in a blender and blend on high speed until very smooth. Serve immediately or store in a jar in the refrigerator for up to 1 week.

LEMON, MINT + ALMOND RELISH

Almost like a rough pesto, I use this to top thick slices of grilled pork tenderloin and wedges of roasted cabbage. It's also wonderful stirred into a bowl of steamed green beans, a pot of cooked rice, or a dish of pureed squash. Or try topping a platter of roasted carrots with spoonfuls of ricotta and then spoonfuls of this. Or just toss it with spaghetti. Or serve with cheese. Or top soup with it (like the Triple Carrot Soup on page 100). It's happy in so many places.

Makes 1 cup [240 ml]

Finely grated zest and juice of 1 large lemon

1 garlic clove, minced

1 large handful fresh mint, finely chopped (a little stem is fine)

½ cup [70 g] unsalted, roasted almonds, finely chopped

½ cup [120 ml] extra-virgin olive oil

1 teaspoon kosher salt

Place all the ingredients in a small bowl and stir together. Serve immediately or store in a jar in the refrigerator for up to 1 week.

ROASTED PEPPER + CORN RELISH

Somewhere between pickled peppers and corn salad, this relish is, like every recipe in this chapter, incredibly handy and can be enjoyed in so many different ways. Tuck it into your next quesadilla or grilled cheese, serve it on top of roast chicken or grilled fish almost like a salsa, put a big spoonful on a plate along with cornbread and slowly cooked greens, or stir it into hot buttered rice. You can also add a pound [453 g] of peeled and deveined shrimp in the pot with the relish, cook just until opaque (about 5 minutes), and serve on top of creamy grits.

Makes 3 cups [720 ml]

Kernels from 3 ears fresh corn [or a 16-ounce (453 g) package frozen corn kernels]

One 7-ounce [198 g] jar roasted red peppers, rinsed, drained, and finely chopped

½ small red onion, finely chopped (about ¼ cup)

2 garlic cloves, minced

¼ cup [60 ml] apple cider vinegar, or to taste

2 tablespoons honey, or to taste

1½ teaspoons kosher salt, or to taste

1 teaspoon celery seeds

½ teaspoon dried red pepper flakes

Place all the ingredients into a small saucepan over high heat. Bring to a boil, turn the heat to low, and simmer until the corn kernels are tender, about 2 minutes.

Turn off the heat and let the mixture cool to room temperature. Season to taste with any additional salt, honey, or vinegar as you like.

Serve immediately or store in a jar in the refrigerator for up to 2 weeks.

8

ELEVEN FAVORITE BREAKFASTS

SLED DOG MUFFINS

My relationship to running changed for the better when I stopped keeping track of my pace. I felt noticeably happier when I let go of any expectation about my speed or lack thereof. I thought of myself as a slow-but-steady snail. I mentioned this to Grace and she wisely told me to pick a more inspiring mascot (nothing against snails). I landed on a sled dog. I kept picturing how sturdy and tough they are and how they always look so proud. Right around this time, I did a road race in Central Park for God's Love We Deliver, a really amazing organization. Grace came with me. Of all the entrances to the park, the one we randomly chose brought us right past the statue of Balto, the famous sled dog. Sometimes even when you don't look for a sign, one appears. These muffins are my favorite thing to eat before I go for a run. They're a little boost of energy and happen to be totally vegan and gluten-free (be sure to use gluten-free rolled oats).

Makes 12

½ cup [120 ml] water

2 tablespoons chia seeds

1½ cups [180 g] rolled oats, plus 1 cup [120 g] for stirring in

1 very ripe banana, peeled

1 cup [227 g] applesauce

½ cup [120 ml] extra-virgin olive oil

2 teaspoons baking powder

1 teaspoon ground cinnamon

½ teaspoon kosher salt

2 tablespoons raspberry jam (or whatever type of jam you like)

Preheat your oven to 350°F [175°C]. Line a 12-compartment standard muffin tin with paper liners.

Place the water in a large bowl with the chia seeds, stir well to combine, and let sit until the chia seeds swell and soften, about 5 minutes.

Meanwhile, place the 1½ cups [180 g] of oats in a food processor and pulse until finely ground, about ten 3-second pulses. Transfer the ground oats to the bowl with the hydrated chia seeds. Don't clean the food processor just yet.

Place the banana, applesauce, and olive oil in the food processor and puree until smooth. Add the mixture to the ground oats along with the remaining 1 cup [120 g] of oats, and the

baking powder, cinnamon, and salt. Stir well until everything is incorporated.

Evenly divide the batter among the cups in the lined muffin tin. Top each muffin with ½ teaspoon jam (as if you were putting cherries on a dozen ice cream sundaes!).

Bake the muffins until firm to the touch and a toothpick tests clean (avoid the jam when testing), about 35 minutes.

Let the muffins cool to room temperature before serving. Leftovers can be stored in an airtight container at room temperature for up to a few days, then split and toasted in a toaster oven or broiler.

L-E-O SCRAMBLE

A staple of Jewish delicatessens, salty lox (L), creamy eggs (E), and sweet browned onions (O) all scrambled together is my idea of breakfast perfection. It stretches a little bit of a special ingredient into a hearty meal. Plus, since the lox is cut small and doesn't need to be in elegant slices for this, feel free to use the more affordable lox "tidbits" if your grocery store sells them (they're the scraps from the big slices). Serve with toasted and cream cheese–slathered bagels or slices of rye or pumpernickel bread.

Serves 4

8 large eggs

½ teaspoon freshly ground black pepper

2 tablespoons extra-virgin olive oil

2 tablespoons unsalted butter

1 large yellow onion, finely diced

4 ounces [113 g] lox, cut into small pieces

2 large scallions, ends trimmed, thinly sliced

Kosher salt

Place the eggs and pepper in a large bowl and whisk vigorously until combined. Reserve them.

Place the olive oil and butter in a large nonstick skillet over medium heat. Once the butter melts, add the onion and cook, stirring now and then, until the onion is browned and tender, about 10 minutes.

Add the beaten eggs, lox, and scallions to the skillet and cook, stirring, until the eggs are just set, about 3 minutes. Season the eggs to taste with salt (they might not need any depending on how salty your lox is).

Serve the scramble immediately.

BREAKFAST NACHOS

One night when I was a kid at sleepaway camp, our counselor told us she couldn't wait to go to sleep so she could wake up and eat breakfast. This tiny moment has stuck with me for all these years and I always think of her when I'm anticipating a really fun breakfast. These nachos inspire that kind of pure enthusiasm. They're fantastic to make for a crowd, whether it's a group of friends spending the weekend together (and quite possibly getting over a hangover) or a bunch of cousins or kids waking up after a sleepover. These nachos really lend themselves to customization and are an excellent place to use up little bits of leftovers (for example, extra black beans, cooked and crumbled sausage or bacon, or roasted vegetables on the nachos themselves, or a random radish or extra scallions in the tomato mixture). These nachos remind me that two big components of healthy eating are flexibility and pleasure. Both of those are essential for feeling good about ourselves.

Serves 6

2 large tomatoes, finely diced

1 avocado, peeled, pitted, and finely diced

3 tablespoons minced red, yellow, or white onion

1 large handful fresh cilantro, finely chopped (a little stem is fine)

3 tablespoons sliced pickled jalapeños (or 1 whole pickled jalapeño), finely chopped

2 tablespoons fresh lime juice

Kosher salt

6 large eggs

1 tablespoon unsalted butter

6 ounces [170 g] tortilla chips (about 6 cups)

1 cup [110 g] coarsely grated sharp cheddar cheese

1 cup [110 g] coarsely grated Monterey Jack cheese

½ cup [120 g] sour cream

Position your oven rack 6 inches [15 cm] from the broiling element and turn the broiler to high.

Place the tomatoes, avocado, onion, cilantro, pickled jalapeños, and lime juice in a large bowl and season with ½ teaspoon kosher salt. Mix gently to combine and season to taste with more salt if needed. Let the mixture sit while you prepare the nachos.

Place the eggs and ½ teaspoon salt in a small bowl and whisk well to combine. Place the butter in a medium nonstick skillet over medium heat. Once it melts, add the beaten eggs and cook, stirring, until the eggs are just set, about 2 minutes. Turn off the heat and reserve the mixture.

Lay the chips in an even layer on a sheet pan and sprinkle evenly with half of the cheddar cheese and half of the Monterey Jack cheese. Evenly divide the scrambled eggs on top of the cheese layer and then evenly sprinkle the rest of the cheese on top of the eggs.

Broil until the cheese is melted, about 2 minutes (but keep an eye on the nachos as broilers vary and yours might take a little less or a little more time).

Top the nachos with the tomato mixture and dollop the sour cream on top. Serve immediately.

EVERYTHING BAGEL HAND PIES

A few years ago, something called "two-ingredient dough" consisting of Greek yogurt and self-rising flour took the internet by storm. Intrigued, I tried it and was pleasantly surprised by how easy it was to make and versatile it was to use. Since not everyone has self-rising flour in their cupboard, I switched it up to include baking soda and salt, and to keep things on the more whole-grain side, I use half all-purpose flour and half whole wheat (you could use all all-purpose if you'd like). The resulting dough is very bagel-like and is approximately one million times easier to make than homemade bagels. My favorite way to use it is for breakfast hand pies, almost like miniature calzones, filled with scrambled eggs and scallions (a nod to scallion cream cheese, an everything bagel's best friend).

Feel free to mix up the filling and use whatever you'd like. For the spices on top, I like the Everything on Everything Salt + Pepper Blend from Jacobsen Salt or the Everything but the Bagel seasoning from Trader Joe's. If you don't have either of those, you can mix 1 teaspoon each sesame seeds, poppy seeds, and onion flakes. Also these freeze well! Which makes a little effort up front reward you whenever you want an amazing on-the-go breakfast (kids love these . . . just saying). You can put them directly from your freezer into your microwave for about 2 minutes, or into a 350°F [175°C] oven or toaster oven for about 15 minutes, to heat up.

Serves 4

For the filling (and the egg wash)
5 large eggs

½ teaspoon kosher salt

1 tablespoon unsalted butter

4 scallions, ends trimmed, thinly sliced

For the dough
½ cup [63 g] all-purpose flour, plus more for your work surface

½ cup [70 g] whole wheat flour

1 teaspoon baking soda

1 teaspoon granulated sugar

½ teaspoon kosher salt

⅔ cup [190 g] plain, full-fat Greek yogurt

To finish: 1 tablespoon everything bagel seasoning (see recipe introduction)

First, preheat your oven to 375°F [190°C].

Line a sheet pan with parchment paper.

Next, make the filling
Place the eggs and salt in a small bowl and whisk well to combine. Place 2 tablespoons of the egg mixture in a small bowl and reserve it (this is your egg wash that you'll use later to brush the hand pies).

Place the butter in a medium nonstick skillet over medium heat. Once it melts, add the remaining beaten eggs and scallions and cook, stirring, until the eggs are just set, about 3 minutes. Transfer the eggs to a plate to stop them from cooking any longer and let them cool to room temperature. Reserve them.

Next, make your dough
Place the flours, baking soda, sugar, and salt in a medium bowl and whisk well to combine. Add the yogurt to the bowl and mix with a wooden spoon until the mixture is crumbly. Switch to your hands and knead the dough directly in the bowl until it's smooth, about a minute of kneading. If the

(continued)

dough sticks too much to your hands, add more flour, 1 tablespoon at a time, until it's no longer sticky. Alternatively, if there are dry crumbs at the bottom of your bowl, add more yogurt, 1 tablespoon at a time, until they're all absorbed.

Next, assemble and bake your hand pies
Lightly flour your work surface and transfer the dough to it. Evenly divide the dough into 4 pieces and form each into a small ball. Dust each ball with flour and press each into a small disc. Lightly dust a rolling pin with flour and use it to roll each piece of dough into a circle measuring about 6 inches [15 cm] in diameter. If the dough sticks to the rolling pin or your work surface, just dust it with more flour.

Evenly divide the cooled egg mixture among the dough circles. Form each dough circle into a half moon, covering the egg mixture. Roll the edges of each hand pie to form a thick edge and then dip the tines of a fork in flour and use it to press the edges of each hand pie (the quick flour dip will keep the tines from sticking). Transfer the pies to the parchment-lined sheet pan.

Brush each pie with some of the reserved egg wash and sprinkle the everything bagel seasoning evenly on each pie. Bake until golden brown, 15 to 18 minutes. Serve hot.

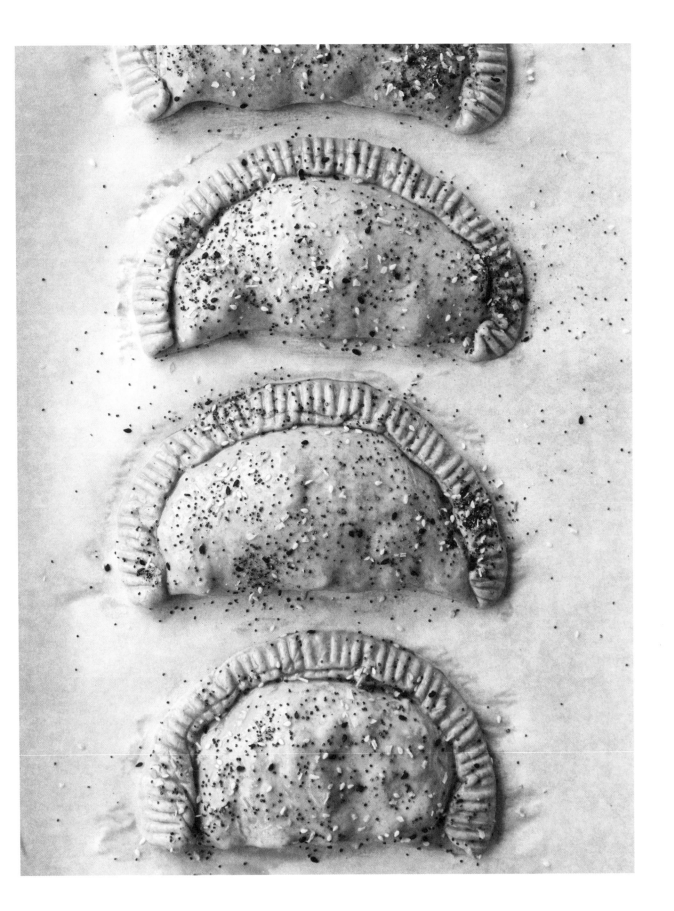

WALNUT "SAUSAGE" PATTIES

This deeply savory, completely vegan mixture mimics the flavor and texture of traditional, meaty breakfast sausage. I like it best alongside the Sweet Potato Hash Browns (page 168) plus some greens and avocado. Or try a patty on your next breakfast sandwich. You can also roll the mixture into balls and roast them for vegan meatballs. If you're gluten-free, be sure to use gluten-free oats.

Serves 4

3 tablespoons extra-virgin olive oil, plus 2 extra tablespoons for cooking the patties

1 small yellow onion, roughly chopped

1 large portobello mushroom, stem discarded, roughly chopped

1 cup [130 g] walnut halves

2 tablespoons minced fresh sage

½ teaspoon pimentón (smoked Spanish paprika)

A few dashes of your favorite hot sauce

1 teaspoon kosher salt, plus a little extra for sprinkling on top

½ cup [60 g] rolled oats

2 tablespoons maple syrup

Place the 3 tablespoons of olive oil in a large nonstick skillet over medium heat and add the onion, portobello, walnuts, sage, pimentón, hot sauce, and salt. Cook, stirring now and then, until the vegetables are just softened and the walnuts are toasted, about 10 minutes. Transfer the contents of the skillet to a food processor and then wipe out the skillet.

Add the oats and maple syrup to the food processor and pulse the mixture until everything is finely chopped and well-combined. Be careful not to overprocess the mixture. You want it to be the texture of ground meat, not a smooth pâté. Season the mixture to taste with salt. Cover and refrigerate for at least 1 hour (and up to 3 days)

to chill it before proceeding (this will help it hold together better).

Divide the mixture into 8 equal portions and form each into a small patty (wetting your hands makes this a little less messy).

Place the remaining 2 tablespoons of oil in the wiped-out skillet and return it to medium heat. Cook the patties, flipping them once, until nicely browned on both sides, about 2 minutes per side. Sprinkle each with a tiny pinch of salt and serve hot.

BEATRICE'S BUBALEH

Even though I never got to meet her, I feel most connected to my grandmother Beatrice's memory when I cook the things she cooked at home and the things she and my grandfather sold at their bakery in Brooklyn. Recently while my mom and I were talking about her mom's cooking, she said, "I forgot about bubaleh! Have I told you about bubaleh?" I thought it was just a Yiddish term of endearment. It turns out it also means wonderful pancakes made of whipped eggs and matzoh meal (finely ground matzoh crackers) that are almost like matzoh balls reimagined as pancakes. My mom described them, I took notes, and then I made them for her. My mom closed her eyes and said, "Just like my mom's." Serve with sour cream, applesauce, and/or jam if you'd like.

Makes four 6-inch [15-cm] pancakes

4 large eggs

½ cup [68 g] matzoh meal

½ teaspoon kosher salt

¼ cup [60 ml] seltzer

2 tablespoons unsalted butter, divided

2 tablespoons sugar

Separate the egg whites and yolks into two separate mixing bowls.

Whisk the egg whites with an electric handheld mixer on high speed (or just a whisk and elbow grease) to form stiff peaks.

Whisk the matzoh meal and salt into the egg yolks and then gently whisk in the seltzer. Gently fold the egg whites into the yolks.

Place ½ tablespoon of the butter in a small nonstick skillet over medium heat. Once the butter melts, add a quarter of the batter and cook until the underside is golden brown and the whole thing holds together, about 2 minutes. Gently flip the bubaleh over and cook until the second side is also browned, about 2 more minutes. Transfer the bubaleh to a plate and repeat the process with the rest of the butter and batter until you've made 4 large pancakes.

Sprinkle the sugar evenly on top of each bubaleh and serve immediately. Bubaleh waits for nobody.

MY GRANDMA BEATRICE, 1920

SWEET POTATO HASH BROWNS

Incredibly simple, these hash browns are made just of onions, peppers, and coarsely grated sweet potatoes. You could use fresh garlic instead of garlic powder, but its flavor feels distinctly diner-y to me and hits just the right note for these hash browns. Serve alongside the Kitchen Sink Frittata (page 171), or enjoy them with the Walnut "Sausage" Patties (page 166) for a completely vegan breakfast. I also love them in a grain bowl with some rice, cooked greens, thinly sliced cucumber, and a drizzle of Go-to Dressing (page 146). Or, as my friend Steph suggested when she tested this recipe for me, use the hash browns as a taco filling.

Serves 4

3 tablespoons extra-virgin olive oil

1 small yellow onion, finely diced

1 small green or red bell pepper, stemmed, seeded, and finely diced

1 pound [453 g] sweet potatoes, coarsely grated (about 1 very large or 2 medium sweet potatoes and there's no need to peel, just give them a good scrub)

1 teaspoon garlic powder

1 teaspoon kosher salt

Place the olive oil in a large nonstick skillet over medium heat. Add the onion and bell pepper and cook, stirring now and then, until beginning to soften, about 8 minutes. Add the sweet potatoes, sprinkle with the garlic powder and salt, and toss everything well to combine.

Spread the mixture into an even layer and cook, without disturbing the hash browns, until they begin to crisp on the bottom, about 5 minutes. This initial undisturbed time helps you get lovely crispy bits in the final hash browns. After your patient waiting, give the hash browns a good stir and to break them up. Continue to cook the hash browns, stirring now and then, until the sweet potatoes are tender and cooked through, an additional 5 minutes. Season to taste with salt and serve immediately.

KITCHEN SINK FRITTATA

The only rule about what goes into a frittata is that there are no rules. Here's the one I most enjoy, with a little sausage, tons of spinach, and plenty of sweet shallots and tiny tomatoes. Feel free to use whatever you have, from salami and goat cheese and arugula, to kale and scallions and leftover roasted potatoes. Anything goes. You can always make the filling ahead of time, hold it in a container in the fridge, and then assemble and bake the frittata whenever you're ready to eat. Or you can bake the whole thing and just warm it up in a 300°F [150°C] oven before serving . . . or just serve it at room temperature. You can also bake the frittata, cut it into wedges, wrap each wedge in plastic wrap (or whatever you use to freeze things in) and freeze them. Then you can unwrap a piece and pop it in the toaster oven or microwave for a quick breakfast before school or work.

Serves 6

2 tablespoons extra-virgin olive oil

½ pound [227 g] fresh breakfast sausage, casings discarded

6 large shallots, thinly sliced into half-moons (or 1 red onion)

5 ounces [141 g] fresh baby spinach

1 large handful cherry tomatoes, halved

6 large eggs

½ teaspoon kosher salt

½ teaspoon freshly ground black pepper

Preheat your oven to 400°F [200°C].

Place the olive oil in medium oven-safe skillet over medium-high heat. Use your hands to break the sausage into small pieces directly into the skillet. Cook, stirring now and then, until browned and crisp, about 10 minutes. Use a slotted spoon to transfer the sausage to a plate and leave the fat in the skillet.

Add the shallots to the skillet and cook, stirring now and then, until just softened, about 8 minutes. Add the spinach and cook, stirring, until wilted, about 1 minute (it will seem like a lot at first, but

it will quickly wilt and you'll find yourself saying "wow, that really turns to nothing!"). Stir in the cherry tomatoes and the reserved sausage. Turn off the heat and hang onto the skillet.

Crack the eggs into a bowl, add the salt and pepper, and whisk well to combine. Pour the eggs evenly over the sausage mixture and put the skillet in the oven. Bake until the eggs are set and the frittata is firm, about 25 minutes. Cut into wedges and serve immediately while hot (or let it sit and serve at room temperature—it's equally good that way).

ROASTED BANANA + SOUR CREAM WAFFLES

Quickly roasting the bananas makes them extra soft and intensifies their flavor and sweetness, which also allows you to skip any additional sugar in the batter for these waffles. Moreover, roasting the bananas in butter means you get melted, ever-so-slightly browned butter in your batter. Flavor, flavor, flavor! Note that the amount of waffles this batter makes depends entirely on the size of your waffle maker and the amount of batter you put in it. With the inexpensive machine I've depended on for about a decade, I get four medium waffles, each quite thick. If Grace and I are very hungry, we can each put two away (and possibly take a nap afterward). If we're not super hungry, and especially if we have the waffles with a side of sausage or fruit or something, one is good. Last note: peanut butter is also a great thing to spread on these!

Makes four 6-inch [15-cm] waffles

3 bananas, peeled (2 broken into large pieces for the batter, 1 sliced for serving)

3 tablespoons unsalted butter, cubed

2 large eggs

1 cup [240 g] sour cream, plus more for serving

2 teaspoons baking powder

½ teaspoon kosher salt

1 teaspoon ground cinnamon

⅛ teaspoon ground cloves

1 cup [140 g] whole wheat flour

Cooking spray (my preference is olive oil spray, but use whatever you have)

Maple syrup, for serving

Preheat your oven to 400°F [200°C].

Place the 2 bananas broken into large pieces and the butter in a small baking dish and roast until the bananas and butter are a little bit browned and the bananas are very soft when you press them with a fork, about 15 minutes.

Turn the oven down to 250°F [120°C] and heat your waffle iron to its highest setting.

Using a fork or a potato masher, crush the bananas directly in their baking dish with the butter.

Transfer the mixture to a large bowl and whisk in the eggs and the sour cream. Whisk in the baking powder, salt, cinnamon, and cloves. Stir in the whole wheat flour. Be careful not to overmix—just stir it until everything is combined.

Spray your waffle iron with cooking spray. Add enough batter to your waffle iron to cover most of the surface area (the exact amount will depend on the size of your waffle iron). Close the waffle iron and cook the waffle until the iron has stopped steaming and the waffle is golden brown and crisp, about 4 minutes, but the exact timing will depend on the heat of your waffle iron and the size of your waffle. Transfer the waffle to a sheet pan and keep it warm in the 250°F [120°C] oven while you repeat the process with the rest of your batter (spray in between waffles as needed).

Serve the waffles warm with the sliced banana, extra sour cream, and maple syrup.

YOGURT WITH ROASTED PINEAPPLE SAUCE + TOASTED COCONUT

My parents ate endless containers of cottage cheese with pineapple when I was growing up (it was the late eighties, what can I say?). This recipe is a throwback to their go-to snack, but it's got some extra interest since the pineapple gets roasted before it gets pureed (so much more flavorful and sweeter without adding more sugar) and the toasted coconut adds crunch and nuttiness. I layer them with yogurt since Grace and I often have yogurt in our fridge, but you can of course use cottage cheese instead. You can also use the pineapple sauce on ice cream, pancakes, or waffles. It's good stuff.

Makes 2 cups [480 ml] pineapple sauce

1 large ripe pineapple, peeled and cored and cut into bite-sized pieces (or one 16-ounce [453 g] package frozen pineapple, defrosted)

½ teaspoon kosher salt

Plain yogurt, whatever type and amount of fat you like (I like all the fat), for serving

Toasted unsweetened coconut flakes, for serving

Preheat your oven to 400°F [200°C].

Place the pineapple in a baking dish, sprinkle with the salt, and toss to coat. Roast until it's softened and browned in spots, about 30 minutes. Let the pineapple cool to room temperature. Transfer the pineapple to a blender or food processor and puree until crushed and almost smooth, but don't let it get too smooth—a little bit of texture is really nice.

To serve, layer the pineapple with yogurt and toasted coconut in small bowls or glasses. Leftover pineapple sauce can be stored in a container in the refrigerator for up to a week.

WHY I LOVE TO VOLUNTEER

GEORGINE + ME, 2017

Whether it's in the stories behind some of my favorite recipes, or in my social media posts, I talk about volunteering a lot. Like cooking at home, it's something I do regularly that I enjoy and highly recommend.

There are a handful of recipes in these pages that are directly related to Angel Food East, the organization where Grace and I have been volunteering weekly for a few years now. There's the Mustardy Cracker Crumb Fish (page 18), devised one day when some frozen fish fillets begged for something crunchy. There's the Blueberry Crumble (page 212) from one day when a local office spent their volunteer day with us and the many extra hands allowed us to send each client home with their own pan of crumble. There's the Cherry + Allspice Sauce (page 153) based on the one I made once when the pork chops we were roasting needed a little *something*. There's Roger's Jambalaya (page 31) from Roger, an integral member of our team. There's the Coffee Crumb Cake for Georgine (page 180), the same Georgine whom this book was written in memory of. She was our friend who we met on our first day at Angel Food East.

I have been volunteering for most of my adult life. When I lived in New York City, I used to have a weekly shift at God's Love We Deliver, the phenomenally impactful organization that provides nearly two million meals a year to folks in and around the city who are too sick to cook for or shop for themselves. When Grace and I moved out of the city, I missed having a shift. Mostly I missed how I felt when my hours were over. It was a combination of useful, purposeful, grounded, and a little physically tired—all things that sometimes feel far away when you're a freelance writer.

So I did what I tell everyone who is interested in volunteering and asks me about it to do: I Googled the word "volunteer" and my zip code. I made a list of organizations, called around, showed up at a few, and figured out which was the best fit. Like any relationship, finding the place where you'd like to volunteer regularly can take a little time.

This search ended at Angel Food East, a nonprofit organization in Kingston, New York. Founded in 1992 with a mission to provide home-delivered meals to residents living with HIV and AIDS, now more than twenty-five years later, Angel Food East is still cooking and delivering meals to clients who are homebound for a variety of reasons, mostly chronic illness, age, or disability. The organization operates out of a kitchen in an Episcopal church. Grace came with me that first day and we've been going together ever since.

That's one reason I love volunteering: doing it with Grace is a way for us to spend time together that's off-line and removed from our day-to-day responsibilities and routines. We've gotten to know each other in this whole new way. And in reason one is also reason two: volunteering regularly removes you, even if only temporarily, from your day-to-day responsibilities and routines. It's a little pause button that puts everything else into perspective. Whenever I'm feeling worked up about something, volunteering pretty much always makes me feel less so. I have never left a shift wishing I hadn't gone.

Reason three I love volunteering: it's made me a better home cook. Cooking a from-scratch meal for our sixty or so clients in our two-hour shift every week has made me more efficient and creative in the kitchen. Just as necessity is the mother of invention, volunteering in a kitchen like Angel Food East's is the mother of resourcefulness. You use what you have. You figure it out. That little bit of spaghetti sauce left over from last week is the base of this week's chili, just as the extra loaves of bread dropped off by a local bakery that are too stale for sandwiches are prime for bread pudding. You make it work. This easygoingness translates well at home. There's pleasure in finding a place for all these bits and pieces.

Reason four I love it: volunteering has taught me how to delegate. In general, I like taking care of everything by myself, especially in the kitchen. In fact, I pride myself on it. But I don't have to peel every potato, trim every chicken thigh, or sprinkle every serving of pasta with cheese for us to have a successful shift at Angel Food East. In fact, if I tried to, the shift would be more than two hours, the likelihood of burnout would increase, and I would probably be all by myself because who wants to work with a controlling micromanager? More hands not only make for a lighter workload, they also make that workload more enjoyable.

It's been a valuable lesson for me to learn and it's been just as important for me to remember that other people are just as capable as I am—or even more so—in the kitchen. Learning this has made me feel more relaxed when something comes up on a Thursday and I can't be there. My team has got it covered. This is not only a relief, it's also reassurance that I will keep showing up because our shift doesn't depend entirely on me. Just like being resourceful, learning to delegate has translated well outside of my volunteering shift.

And reason number five I love volunteering: it makes me feel connected to my community. We would have never met Georgine had we not showed up at Angel Food East. Or our friend Diane, who we pick up and drop off each week. We wouldn't have met Roger of Roger's Jambalaya (page 31), or Cheryl, who manages the kitchen, or had more time with our friend Karina, who joined our shift. We wouldn't have gotten to serve our clients and hear about their needs and feel like there was something tangible we could do to help. As Georgine always said, I often feel like I get more than I give when I volunteer.

GEORGINE + GRACE, 2018

ME, GRACE + DIANE, 2018

COFFEE CRUMB CAKE FOR GEORGINE

Our friend Georgine passed away in January 2019 at ninety years young. Getting to know her during her final chapter is one of the biggest gifts Grace and I have ever received. She was so spirited, so funny, and always offered us so much perspective. She often said "baking is my Valium" and would share her creations with us. I make this coffee crumb cake, a version of the one she regularly made, with less sugar than she called for and a bit of whole wheat flour in both the cake and the topping. Even if it's not her exact recipe, baking it is the simplest way I know to bring her spirit into my kitchen. Doing so helps me remember that evoking memories is one of the healthiest things that food, any food, can offer us.

Serves about 12

For the cake

Cooking spray (my preference is olive oil spray, but use whatever you have)

2 cups [250 g] all-purpose flour

1 cup [140 g] whole wheat flour

1 tablespoon baking powder

½ teaspoon kosher salt

½ cup [120 ml] canola oil (or other neutral oil such as vegetable)

1 cup [200 g] granulated sugar

2 large eggs

2 teaspoons vanilla extract

1½ cups [360 ml] buttermilk (shake well before measuring!)

For the crumbs

1 cup [125 g] all-purpose flour

1 cup [140 g] whole wheat flour

¾ cup [150 g] granulated sugar

2 teaspoons baking powder

1 tablespoon ground cinnamon

1 teaspoon kosher salt

1 cup [2 sticks, aka 16 tablespoons, aka 227 g] unsalted butter, at room temperature

For serving

Powdered sugar

First, preheat your oven to 350°F [175°C]. Coat a 9-by-13 inch [23-by-33 cm] baking dish with cooking spray.

Next, make the cake batter
Place the flours, baking powder, and salt in a medium bowl and whisk well to combine.

In a separate bowl, whisk together the canola oil, sugar, eggs, vanilla, and buttermilk. Stir the dry ingredients into the wet ingredients and then transfer the batter to the prepared baking dish. Use a spoon or rubber spatula to smooth the top.

Then, make the crumbs
Place the flours, sugar, baking powder, cinnamon, and salt in a large bowl and whisk well to combine.

Add the butter and mix to form large crumbs. The best tools for this job are your clean hands. Just rub the mixture between your fingertips to form crumbs the size of marbles (it's okay if some are finer). Evenly sprinkle the crumb mixture on top of the cake batter (it will be a thick layer).

Bake and serve
Bake until the crumbs are golden brown and a toothpick inserted all the way through the crumbs and into the cake tests clean, 40 to 45 minutes.

Let the cake cool completely to room temperature. Dust with powdered sugar, cut into squares, and serve. Leftovers can be stored in an airtight container at room temperature for a couple of days (good luck with that . . . this cake goes fast!).

9

TEN NOSHES + A DRINK

WHITE BEAN + PIMENTÓN DIP

RED LENTIL SOUP DIP

WHITE BEAN + PIMENTÓN DIP

Made with ingredients I always have on hand, this dip is the thing I make when we have people coming around and I've forgotten to prepare something to have before the meal, or when I need a little snack in between lunch and dinner. It's also totally vegan and gluten-free if that's important to you. Serve this with crackers, sliced raw or barely steamed vegetables, or toasted pita bread (or any type of toast). Or spread it on a roll and layer with avocado, tomato, and cheddar for an excellent vegetarian sandwich. Leftovers can be stored in a covered container in the fridge for up to three days. Leftovers can also be turned into white bean soup by heating them up with vegetable or chicken stock.

Makes about 2 cups [480 ml]

2 garlic cloves

Two 15-ounce [425 g] cans white beans, rinsed and drained

2 teaspoons pimentón (smoked Spanish paprika), plus a little extra for sprinkling on top

1 teaspoon kosher salt, plus more as needed

½ cup [120 ml] extra-virgin olive oil, plus extra for drizzling on top

2 tablespoons fresh lemon juice (or sherry vinegar)

Set your food processor up and turn it on and, while it's spinning, drop the garlic cloves through the opening at the top and run the machine until they're minced, about 10 seconds. Letting them hit the blade while it's already spinning keeps them from getting stuck and guarantees that you won't get a big piece of raw garlic in your final dip. You can also mince the garlic with a knife first.

Add the remaining ingredients to the food processor and puree until smooth. Scrape down the sides if needed.

If you don't have a food processor, you can use a blender, but start with minced garlic and with half of the beans. Once they are super smooth with the oil and everything, add the remaining beans (I find if I do it all at once, the blender gets stuck).

Season the dip to taste with salt and then transfer it to a shallow bowl. Drizzle a little olive oil (about 1 tablespoon or so) on top of the dip, sprinkle with a little extra pimentón, and serve immediately.

RED LENTIL SOUP DIP

Even though I wrote a whole cookbook about reinventing leftovers, called *Now & Again*, I often eat tons of stuff cold, straight out of the container. We all contain multitudes. Enter this dip, which is inspired by leftover red lentil soup that I mistook for hummus one day and stuck a carrot into and ate standing in front of my refrigerator. It was so good that I decided to do it on purpose going forward and cook red lentils as if I were going to turn them into a gently spiced soup, in the spirit of traditional masoor dal, but on the thicker side with less liquid. Serve with raw vegetables, or any type of cracker (it's especially good with papadums), or put a dollop onto a bowl of rice and cooked vegetables and call it lunch. And you can always add a few cups of stock, serve it warm, and call it . . . soup.

Makes about 2 cups [480 ml]

3 tablespoons coconut oil (or extra-virgin olive oil)

2 teaspoons garam masala (or ½ teaspoon each ground cumin, coriander, turmeric, and black pepper)

½ cup [100 g] split red lentils

One 13½-ounce [400 ml] can coconut milk

1 teaspoon kosher salt

2 tablespoons plain yogurt (or coconut milk yogurt if you're vegan), for serving

2 tablespoons toasted unsweetened coconut flakes, for serving

Place the coconut oil and garam masala in a medium saucepan over medium heat. When the spices begin to smell fragrant, just about 30 seconds, stir in the lentils, coconut milk, and salt. Bring the mixture to a boil, turn the heat to low, cover the pot, and simmer until the lentils are completely soft, 20 to 25 minutes. Season the mixture to taste with salt.

Turn off the heat and let the mixture cool to room temperature. It will thicken slightly as it cools. Transfer the dip to a serving bowl. Top with the yogurt and toasted coconut and serve immediately.

HONEYED APRICOTS WITH CREAM CHEESE + PISTACHIOS

Easy peasy, these stuffed apricots are inspired by kaymaklı kayısı tatlısı, the traditional Turkish sweet made with dried apricots soaked in lemony syrup, stuffed with creamy cheese (often made with buffalo milk), and coated in crunchy nuts. They're not only adorable, they're also just the thing to make a meal last a little longer, or to fill the space after school or work but before dinner is ready. The apricot-infused, honey-sweetened liquid left over from poaching the apricots is worth holding onto. Use it in your next pitcher of iced tea, mix it with whiskey or bourbon and ice for an easy cocktail, or soak some day-old pound cake in it and serve with whipped cream. If you can't find salted, roasted pistachio kernels, just use unsalted ones and add a pinch of salt.

Makes 12

1 cup [240 ml] water

Finely grated zest and juice of 1 large lemon

3 tablespoons honey

12 large dried apricots

½ cup [113 g] cream cheese, at room temperature

3 tablespoons salted, roasted pistachio kernels, finely chopped

Place the water, lemon zest and juice, honey, and apricots in a small saucepan over high heat. Bring to a boil and then turn off the heat. Let the apricots cool to room temperature.

Drain the apricots (see recipe introduction for ideas on what to do with the liquid) and then split each one open without entirely separating the halves (leave one side attached . . . this is almost like opening up a pita bread). Evenly divide the cream cheese among the apricots. Roll the exposed cream cheese part of each apricot in the chopped pistachios.

Serve immediately (or cover and store at room temperature for up 1 hour, or in the refrigerator for up to 2 days; serve at room temperature).

AUNT RENEE'S GEFILTE BITES

My aunt Renee cooked huge amounts of food whenever she cooked. If she was only expecting two people, she'd cook for twenty. Even the curtains in her Brooklyn apartment smelled like chicken soup. I particularly loved her gefilte fish, which I always thought was lighter than any other. For anyone uninitiated to this Ashkenazi classic, gefilte fish is basically a large poached fish meatball, and it can lean toward dense (which is putting it diplomatically). When my aunt Renee got sick toward the end of her life, I started asking her about all of her recipes. When we got to her gefilte fish, her answer shocked me. "It's from the store, Julia," she said. Sometimes even legends take shortcuts.

I developed these gefilte bites, basically bite-sized roasted fish meatballs (but doesn't "gefilte bites" sound more fun?) with my aunt Renee in mind. I think she would've gotten a kick out of them. Served with horseradish mayonnaise for dipping, they're an unexpected and very nostalgia-inducing appetizer and a fun thing to shake up your next Passover Seder. If you don't have matzoh meal (ground matzoh crackers), feel free to use breadcrumbs or finely crushed crackers (if you do this, just keep in mind that they won't be Kosher for Passover).

Makes 20

For the gefilte bites

1 small yellow onion, roughly chopped

1 large celery stalk, roughly chopped

1 large carrot, peeled and roughly chopped

1 pound [453 g] boneless, skinless white fish (such as cod, haddock, grouper, or halibut), cut into bite-sized pieces

1 large egg, lightly beaten

1 teaspoon kosher salt

½ teaspoon freshly ground black pepper

2 tablespoons minced fresh dill

⅓ cup [45 g] matzoh meal

For the dipping sauce

¼ cup [60 g] mayonnaise

2 tablespoons prepared horseradish, preferably the red kind with beets

¼ teaspoon kosher salt

First, make the gefilte bites
Preheat your oven to 425°F [220°C]. Line a sheet pan with parchment paper and set it aside.

Place the onion, celery, and carrot in the bowl of a food processor and pulse until very finely chopped. Add the fish and pulse until it's finely chopped (be mindful not to overprocess and turn this into a paste—you just want the fish to be finely chopped, almost like it were ground meat). If you don't have

a food processor, you can just finely chop the vegetables and the fish by hand.

Transfer the fish mixture to a large bowl and stir in the egg, salt, black pepper, dill, and matzoh meal. Mix everything well to combine (your hands are the best tool for this job).

Form the mixture into 20 even balls. It's helpful to divide the mixture in half and then in half again and so on to make sure they're all the same size. Wetting your hands with cold water will help keep the mixture from sticking to them.

Evenly space the gefilte bites on the prepared sheet pan and roast until they're firm to the touch, about 25 minutes. Let the gefilte bites rest for at least 10 minutes before transferring to a serving platter.

Next, make the sauce
While the gefilte bites rest, place the mayonnaise, prepared horseradish, and salt in a small bowl and whisk well to combine.

And serve
Serve the gefilte bites warm or at room temperature with toothpicks for easy eating and the horseradish mixture for dipping.

MY AUNT RENEE, MOM,
ME + MY AUNT DEBBY, 2000

Sweet + Salty Sesame Peanuts

The scent of toasted nuts caramelizing in honey and sugar that wafts from the Nuts4Nuts carts that dot New York City is one of the smells I most associate with my twenty years living in the city. Alejandro Rad started the brand in 1993 with one cart and a recipe from Argentina, where he was born, and he now owns the company with Cliff Stanton and they supply nearly one hundred carts throughout the city. The carts are known for their copper bowls, which vendors use to coat the nuts with a sweet, crunchy coating. Each order comes in its own little wax paper bag. When I was a little kid in downtown Manhattan, I loved eating them on the walk home from school, thrilled to have my own tiny package that I didn't have to share. I used to occasionally get them in college, far uptown, and during my early twenties when I returned downtown and wanted a reminder of something from years ago. Now that I live outside of the city, I make a version of the peanuts for myself that's light on the sugary coating, generous on salt to balance the sweet, and filled with sesame for extra flavor. A little lime juice at the end adds brightness. Serve these with your favorite cocktail, wine, beer, or just a tall iced tea. They're also great on top of a bowl of rice and vegetables.

Makes 1 cup [115 g]

1 cup [115 g] roasted, unsalted peanuts (if they're salted, just skip the extra salt)

1 tablespoon sesame seeds

1 teaspoon toasted sesame oil

½ teaspoon granulated sugar

½ teaspoon kosher salt

Half of a fresh lime

Place the peanuts, sesame seeds, sesame oil, sugar, and salt in a small skillet over medium heat. Cook, stirring, until everything is very fragrant and the sesame seeds start to brown, about 3 minutes.

Transfer to a serving bowl. Squeeze the lime evenly over the peanuts. Serve immediately (if you don't serve these straightaway, wait to squeeze the lime on top until just before serving).

SPINACH + POTATO BITES

Dr. Praeger's, purveyors of old-school veggie burgers and other frozen favorites, makes these bite-sized, animal-shaped spinach nugget things that Grace adores. She often pops them in our toaster oven and eats them with ketchup and is just so happy. These are a homemade version of those and are great not only for adults, but especially for kids. You cook a little bit of potato and a lot of spinach, blitz them with onion and a couple of other things, and then pour it onto a sheet pan and bake the whole thing for a while to remove most of the moisture. You're left with a gigantic sheet that can be cut out with cookie cutters into animal shapes (any shape, really), or simply cut into squares. Like the original, you can prepare the bites, freeze them on a tray, and then keep them in the freezer in a container or plastic bag and then just heat them up in a 400°F [200°C] oven (or toaster oven) when you want a fun snack. Ketchup is great, but also feel free to serve these with something else, like Parmesan + Peppercorn Dressing (page 146), Creamy Feta + Scallion Dressing (page 147), or Creamy Miso + Cashew Dressing (page 149).

Serves 4 as a snack

Cooking spray (my preference is olive oil spray, but use whatever you have)

1 large baking potato [about ¾ pound (340 g)], peeled and roughly chopped

5 ounces [141 g] fresh baby spinach

1 small yellow or white onion, roughly chopped

3 tablespoons cornstarch

2 teaspoons kosher salt

½ teaspoon garlic powder

1 large egg

Preheat your oven to 400°F [200°C]. If you have quarter sheet pan [9-by-13-inch (23-by-33-cm)], use it—it's the best thing to make these. If you don't have one of those, use a regular sheet pan. You can also use a baking dish. Whatever baking vessel you use, line it with a piece of parchment paper and spray it with cooking spray (or rub 1 teaspoon of olive oil on the surface of the paper). Doing this two-step process will go a long way to prevent a stuck-on mess later.

Place the chopped potato in a medium pot and cover with cold water. Set over high heat and bring to a boil, then lower the heat and simmer until the potato is tender and can be easily pierced with a paring knife, about 15 minutes. Add the spinach to the pot (it might seem like a lot, but it will quickly wilt) and stir until it's totally wilted and collapsed,

about 30 seconds. Drain the vegetables in a colander and give them a very good shake until they're dry.

Place the onion in the bowl of a food processor and pulse until finely chopped. Add the thoroughly drained potatoes and spinach and pulse until the potato is completely pureed and the spinach is finely chopped and incorporated (stop to scrape down the sides of the food processor as needed to keep everything consistent).

Place the cornstarch, salt, and garlic powder in a small bowl, stir them together, and then add them to the potato mixture (mixing them first helps to make sure they're evenly distributed). Pulse until combined. Crack the egg into the mixture and pulse again until combined.

Pour the mixture onto your prepared baking vessel. If you're using a quarter sheet pan or similarly sized baking dish, use a rubber spatula to spread the mixture into an even layer. If you're using a larger vessel, like a regular sheet pan, spread the mixture into a roughly 9-by-13-inch [23-by-33-cm] rectangle. You want it to be about ½ inch [1 cm] thick.

Bake until the mixture is quite dried out, a little brown on top, and firm, about 50 minutes. Set the sheet pan on a rack to cool for at least 15 minutes (or longer, until it's room temperature).

Pick up the edges of the parchment and transfer the whole thing to a cutting board. Use a cookie cutter to cut shapes out (any shapes you'd like!) or just use a chef's knife to cut into 24 even, bite-sized pieces. Serve warm or at room temperature. Leftovers can be refrigerated for up to few days or frozen for up to a few months. Either way, warm in a hot oven before enjoying.

PARSNIP LATKES

Grace and I live near a small farm called Long Season Farm, and wife-and-husband team Erin and Sam grow the most beautiful produce (you can "meet" them on page 231). We're so happy to be part of their CSA (which stands for "community-supported agriculture," and many farms offer a CSA program; you pay your farmer up front and then get all sorts of produce throughout the season). Once we got so many parsnips in our CSA share and I was getting tired of roasting vegetables (always a good idea, but sometimes you get bored), so I decided to grate them and turn them into crispy little latkes. Grace and I ate nearly the whole batch in one sitting.

I've come to love these as an alternative to potato latkes because parsnips are sweet and nutty, plus they also have less moisture than potatoes, so you don't have to worry about getting rid of their moisture (nothing worse than a soggy latke). This recipe also works well with grated sweet potatoes or carrots. If you want to make these ahead, you can prepare them a few hours before you plan to eat them, set them on a cookie cooling rack on top of a sheet pan and keep them at room temperature, and then warm them in a 350°F [175°C] oven for a few minutes when you're ready to eat.

Makes about 18

¼ cup [31 g] all-purpose flour

½ teaspoon baking powder

1½ teaspoons kosher salt, plus more for serving

1 pound [453 g] parsnips, ends trimmed, peeled, and coarsely grated (about 6 medium parsnips or 4 cups grated)

2 large eggs, lightly beaten

¼ cup [60 ml] extra-virgin olive oil, plus more as needed

Sour cream and applesauce, for serving (optional, but recommended)

Place the flour, baking powder, and salt in a large bowl and whisk well to combine. Add the grated parsnips and the eggs and stir everything well to combine.

Line a plate with paper towels and reserve it.

Place the olive oil in a large nonstick skillet over medium-high heat. Once the oil is hot (a little bit of the latke mixture will sizzle upon contact), drop heaping tablespoonfuls of the batter into the skillet, without crowding them, and use the back of the spoon to press each mound into a flat pancake. Cook the latkes until the undersides are browned, about 3 minutes, then carefully turn them and cook until the second sides are nicely browned, about 2 minutes.

Transfer the latkes to the prepared plate and fry the remaining batter in batches, adding more oil to the pan if necessary. Sprinkle the warm latkes with a tiny pinch of salt. Serve immediately with sour cream and applesauce for topping (if using).

PORK + PINEAPPLE TOOTHPICKS

Inspired by both Hawaiian pizza and tacos al pastor, these little skewers of sweet, juicy pineapple and sticky glazed pork are the best way I know to turn a single pork chop into a dozen hors d'oeuvres. And consider yourself warned: the pork has got a little kick. If you prefer things less spicy, just use less chili garlic sauce (or, conversely, increase it if you want things hotter). You can also multiply the recipe, mix the pineapple into the skillet right at the end, and serve the mix over rice or noodles and call it dinner.

Makes 1 dozen bites

1 tablespoon canola oil (or other neutral oil such as vegetable)

One 8-ounce [227 g] boneless pork chop, cut into a dozen bite-sized pieces

¼ teaspoon kosher salt

1 tablespoon soy sauce

1 tablespoon chili garlic sauce (such as sambal)

1 tablespoon light brown sugar

12 bite-sized cubes fresh pineapple

Place the canola oil in a medium nonstick skillet over medium-high heat. Add the pork pieces, season them with the salt, and cook, turning them a couple of times as they cook, until browned all over, about 4 minutes.

Add the soy sauce, chili garlic sauce, and brown sugar to the skillet. Stir everything together until the pork is beautifully glazed, about 30 seconds. Turn off the heat.

Stab each piece of pork with a toothpick and then follow that up with a piece of pineapple (this way the pineapple will absorb any juices from the pork). Serve immediately.

BUFFALO BRUSSELS SPROUTS

Roasted in a super-hot oven until crisp, tossed with butter and hot sauce, and then topped with Gorgonzola and thinly sliced celery, these Brussels sprouts are about as far away from mushy and dull as you can get. If you don't like things too spicy, start with less hot sauce (and feel free to add more to taste if you prefer things super spicy). Serve with toothpicks for easy noshing, or they also work well as a side dish.

Serves 4

1½ pounds [680 g] Brussels sprouts, tough outer leaves trimmed

3 tablespoons extra-virgin olive oil

½ teaspoon kosher salt, plus more as needed

3 tablespoons unsalted butter, melted

2 tablespoons hot sauce (I like Frank's RedHot for this)

⅓ cup [35 g] crumbled Gorgonzola cheese

1 large celery stalk, thinly sliced (on the diagonal if you're feeling fancy!), plus a few celery leaves for garnish if you have them and feel like it (not a deal breaker if not!)

Preheat your oven to 450°F [230°C].

Place the Brussels sprouts on a sheet pan. Drizzle with the olive oil, sprinkle with the salt, and mix everything together with your hands.

Roast the sprouts, stirring them once or twice while they cook, until they're softened (test with a paring knife) and also dark brown and crispy, about 20 minutes.

Meanwhile, place the melted butter and hot sauce in a large bowl and stir well to combine.

Transfer the hot sprouts to the butter mixture and toss well to combine. Season the sprouts to taste with additional salt if needed.

Transfer the sprouts to a serving platter. Sprinkle evenly with the cheese, celery, and celery leaves. Serve hot.

ZUCCHINI, GREEN OLIVE + FETA FRITTERS

Ever find yourself with a ton of zucchini and no idea what to do with it? Fritter it. I've never met a zucchini fritter I didn't love, and these, filled with chopped olives and salty feta cheese, might just be my favorite. If you're making these for a party or something like that, feel free to make them ahead and then warm them on a cookie cooling rack set on top of a sheet pan in a 400°F [200°C] oven until hot and crisp. They're also good at room temperature. Not only are these a great nosh, they're also wonderful tucked into a pita bread with some hummus and pickled vegetables or as part of a vegetarian spread (maybe alongside the Shiitake + Pumpkin Biryani, page 72, and the Braised Red Cabbage + Green Apples, page 136). Also consider this recipe a template that you can fill in however you like. Use a different type of olive or maybe a caper, switch up the cheese, add some herbs to the fritters or the yogurt sauce. Go nuts! Add nuts!

Makes 12

For the sauce

½ cup [120 g] full-fat plain yogurt (preferably regular yogurt, not thick Greek yogurt)

1 tablespoon fresh lemon juice

1 garlic clove, minced

¼ teaspoon kosher salt

For the fritters

¼ cup [31 g] all-purpose flour

2 tablespoons cornstarch

½ teaspoon baking powder

½ teaspoon kosher salt, plus more for sprinkling on top

1 large zucchini [about ½ pound (227 g)], ends trimmed, coarsely grated

¼ cup [60 g] pitted green olives, roughly chopped

¾ cup [80 g] crumbled feta cheese

1 large egg, lightly beaten

¼ cup [60 ml] extra-virgin olive oil, plus more as needed

First, make the sauce
Place the yogurt, lemon juice, garlic, and salt in a small bowl and whisk well to combine. Reserve the mixture.

Next, make the fritters
Place the flour, cornstarch, baking powder, and salt in a large bowl and whisk well to combine.

Place the zucchini in a clean kitchen towel and wring it out over the sink to remove the excess moisture. Transfer the squeezed zucchini to the bowl with the flour mixture and add the olives, feta, and egg. Stir everything well to combine.

Line a plate with a paper towels and reserve it.

Place the olive oil in a large nonstick skillet over medium-high heat. Once the oil is hot (a little bit of the fritter mixture will sizzle upon contact), drop tablespoonfuls of the batter into the skillet, without crowding them, and use the back of the spoon to press each mound into a flat pancake. Cook the fritters until the undersides are browned, about 3 minutes, then carefully turn them and cook until the second sides are nicely browned, about 2 minutes. Transfer the fritters to the prepared plate and fry the remaining batter in batches, adding more oil to the pan if necessary. Sprinkle the warm fritters with a tiny pinch of salt.

And serve
Serve the fritters immediately, with the yogurt sauce for dipping. If you'd like, cut the rest of the lemon you used for the sauce into wedges for squeezing over the fritters.

JENNIE + ME ON MY BIRTHDAY, 1990-ish

JENNIE + MY MOM,
JENNIE'S 60th, 2015

JENNIE'S SORREL

For the past few years Jennie, my childhood babysitter, has spent Thanksgiving with us at our house. Along with homemade bread and a rum cake, there is always a bag of sorrel in her suitcase when she arrives. Not to be confused with the green herb also called sorrel, the sorrel Jennie carries with her refers to dried hibiscus flowers, the same ones that are ground for hibiscus tea bags. Widely available in Caribbean grocery stores and online (and also in stores that stock Mexican ingredients under the name "jamaica"), sorrel is also the name of the drink that's prepared with it. Jennie brews hers with tons of fresh ginger and dried clove and barely sweetens it. We put the pitcher out next to lots of mix-ins. Some people just drink it straight, some mix it with seltzer, others with sparkling wine, and some, like Jennie says, "spike it way up" with rum, gin, tequila, or vodka. It's the perfect something-for-everyone drink, and it always reminds me of one of my favorite people in the entire world.

Serves 10

2 ounces [57 g] red sorrel (dried hibiscus flowers)

One 3-inch [7-cm] piece fresh ginger, peeled and roughly chopped

1 tablespoon whole cloves

10 cups [2.3 liters] water

¼ cup [50 g] granulated sugar, plus more if you'd like

Ice, for serving

Place the sorrel in a sieve and rinse well with cold tap water. Transfer the sorrel to a medium pot and add the ginger, cloves, and water. Set the pot over high heat and bring the mixture to a boil. Let it boil for 5 minutes, turn off the heat, stir in the sugar, and cover the pot. Let the mixture steep until it cools to room temperature before serving (you can let it sit overnight if you'd like, which intensifies the flavor).

Taste the sorrel and stir in more sugar if you'd like. Strain the mixture through a sieve into a pitcher. Serve over ice.

10

ELEVEN MEMORABLE SWEETS

CARD NIGHT GINGER COOKIES

I always think of Amelia, Cleo, and Lizzy, three of my closest friends, as my "Card Night" friends. We used to all live in New York and would get together to make dinner and then play cards. Then we started just making dinner. Then, one by one, we all left the city. Yet, we still find ways to keep the glue between us. We've navigated not only moves, but also children and marriages and new jobs and old jobs and loss together. No matter what, we laugh so much together. And we talk about what we're cooking all of the time.

These cookies, a version of the ones Amelia showed up with one night in our early days (back when we used to actually play cards!), make me think of my Card Night friends. Each time I make them, I'm filled with love. I hope they bring you that same feeling. Note that these are the best cookies EVER to use for homemade ice cream sandwiches.

Makes 20

For the cookies
1¼ cups [156 g] all-purpose flour

1¼ cups [175 g] whole wheat flour

2 teaspoons baking soda

1½ tablespoons ground ginger

½ teaspoon ground cinnamon

½ teaspoon ground cloves

½ teaspoon kosher salt

¾ cup unsalted butter [1½ sticks, aka 12 tablespoons, aka 170 g], at room temperature (if you didn't manage to take it out of the fridge in time to soften, simply cut it into small pieces and microwave in 5-second intervals until it's soft but not melted)

½ cup [100 g] granulated sugar

½ cup [120 ml] molasses

1 large egg

For coating the cookies
3 tablespoons granulated sugar

½ teaspoon ground cinnamon

First, preheat your oven to 350°F [175°C].

Line 2 sheet pans with parchment paper.

Next, make the cookie dough
Place the flours, baking soda, ginger, cinnamon, cloves, and salt in a medium bowl and whisk well to combine.

Place the butter and sugar in a separate bowl and use an electric handheld mixer on high speed (or an electric stand mixer or just a wooden spoon and a lot of elbow grease) to mix the butter and sugar together until light and fluffy, a solid 2 minutes of mixing with a couple of quick pauses to scrape the bowl. Beat in the molasses and then the egg.

Use a wooden spoon to stir the flour mixture into the butter mixture.

Divide the dough into 20 even pieces. The best way to do this is to use your clean hands or a spoon to divide the dough in half, then divide that half in half, and so on until you end up with 20 pieces. Use your hands to roll each piece into a small ball. You can use one of the prepared sheet pans as a landing pad for the cookies as you roll them.

Then make the cookie coating
Place the sugar and cinnamon in a small bowl and stir well to combine.

And coat and bake the cookies

Roll each dough ball into the cinnamon sugar mixture and then evenly space the dough balls on the sheet pans (10 per tray with space between them). Gently pat each dough ball down just a smidge.

Bake the cookies, rotating the trays halfway through baking, until the cookies spread a little and start to crack on top, about 10 minutes total (rotate the trays after 5 minutes). They will still be a little soft, but keep in mind that cookies crisp as they cool.

Set the pans on a cookie cooling rack and allow the cookies to cool to room temperature before eating (if you can).

Some cookie logistics to keep in mind

Any leftovers can be stored in an airtight container at room temperature for up to a few days.

Baked cookies can also be frozen in a freezer bag for up to 2 months and warmed in a 300°F [150°C] oven for a few minutes before enjoying.

You can make the dough ahead of time, roll it into balls, and then refrigerate for up to 3 days or freeze for up to 2 months (defrost before baking) and then roll in cinnamon sugar and bake (give the cookies a few extra minutes if baking from cold).

CLEO, AMELIA, LIZZY + ME, 2019
(WITH TALLULAH + THOMAS!)

APRICOT + ALMOND BISCOTTI

Made with almond flour (which keeps them gluten-free), roasted almonds, and a tiny bit of almond extract, these adorable, barely sweet cookies are for my mother, who loves almond anything. Apricot preserves and chopped dried apricots provide all the sugar in the recipe, which means there's flavor with the sweetness, which means you get the most bang for your sugar buck. Serve with tea or coffee.

Makes 18

2 large eggs

½ cup [165 g] apricot preserves

¼ teaspoon almond extract

3 tablespoons extra-virgin olive oil

2 tablespoons cornstarch

½ teaspoon baking soda

½ teaspoon kosher salt

2 cups [220 g] almond flour

½ cup [70 g] roasted, salted almonds

½ cup [100 g] dried apricots, roughly chopped

Preheat your oven to 350°F [175°C]. Line a sheet pan with parchment paper and set it aside.

Place the eggs, preserves, almond extract, and olive oil in a large bowl and whisk well to combine. Add the cornstarch, baking soda, and salt and whisk well to make sure those are incorporated really well. Stir in the almond flour and then fold in the almonds and apricots. The dough will be sticky, almost more of an extremely thick batter.

Use a rubber spatula to scrape the dough onto the prepared sheet pan. Wet your hands (to prevent the dough from sticking to them) and use them to shape the dough into a 12-by-3-inch [30-by-8-cm] rectangle. Bake the loaf until it is golden brown and firm to the touch, about 30 minutes.

Remove the loaf from the oven and carefully transfer it to a cutting board (you can let it cool down a bit first if you'd like, but I am impatient).

Use a serrated knife to cut the loaf into 18 cookies, each measuring about ½ inch [1 cm] thick. I always trim off the ends and snack on them and so should you. No one needs to know.

Lay the cookies on one of their cut sides on the still-warm sheet pan and bake until the exposed sides are dried out a bit, about 3 minutes. Carefully turn each cookie over and bake until the second sides are also dried out a bit, about another 3 minutes. Transfer the cookies to a rack to cool (they will crisp more as they cool). Serve at room temperature.

Leftovers can be stored in a tightly covered container at room temperature for up to 3 days or frozen for up to 1 month or so (let them defrost at room temperature and serve as is, or re-crisp them in the oven doing 3 minutes per side like when you first baked them).

ORANGE + GREEK YOGURT CAKE

With creamy Greek yogurt, fresh orange juice and zest, and tons of vanilla extract, this simple loaf cake gives you all the notes of a Creamsicle. I love serving it in slices topped with extra yogurt and sliced oranges, but it's also great on its own with tea or coffee for breakfast or an afternoon snack. This is a great thing to gift to a neighbor, or to use to say thank you to someone with more than words (for example, leave a wrapped loaf in your mailbox with a note for whoever delivers your mail).

Serves 8

Cooking spray (my preference is olive oil spray, but use whatever you have)

2 large eggs

1 cup [227 g] full-fat plain Greek yogurt, plus additional for serving

½ cup [120 ml] extra-virgin olive oil

Finely grated zest and juice from 1 large orange, plus an additional orange, peeled and sliced, for serving

1 tablespoon vanilla extract

⅔ cup [133 g] granulated sugar

2 teaspoons baking powder

½ teaspoon kosher salt

1 cup [125 g] all-purpose flour

1 cup [140 g] whole-wheat flour

Preheat your oven to 350°F [175°C].

Coat a 9-by-5-inch [23-by-12-cm] loaf pan with cooking spray.

Place the eggs in a large bowl and whisk well to combine. Add the yogurt, olive oil, orange zest and orange juice, vanilla, sugar, baking powder, and salt and whisk incredibly well until everything is well incorporated. Stir in the flours. Transfer the batter to the prepared loaf pan and use a spoon to spread the batter so that it's in an even layer.

Bake until firm to the touch and a toothpick tests clean, about 55 minutes.

Let the loaf cool to room temperature, then remove it from its pan. Cut into 8 even slices and serve each with a dollop of yogurt and some sliced oranges. Or skip those toppings and just serve the slices plain.

BLUEBERRY CRUMBLE

This crumble was born of a stocked pantry and some extra hands. One day at Angel Food East a group of ten extra volunteers came in and I was put in charge of them. We quickly breezed through the tasks on our list and still had an hour left in our two-hour-long shift. There were a few pounds of blueberries in the freezer and some baking supplies in the pantry. We all whipped up a few trays of this crumble and sent a big portion to each of our sixty clients. The crumble came together so easily and quickly that I had to share it here. Feel free to make it with any type of fruit you like, whether a mix of berries, or berries and stone fruit (blueberries and plums are good friends), or thinly sliced apples. Serve warm or at room temperature with vanilla ice cream or whipped cream. Or enjoy cold in the morning with yogurt.

Serves 6

For the blueberries

1 pound [453 g] fresh or frozen blueberries (if frozen, no need to defrost)

2 tablespoons fresh lemon juice

2 tablespoons cornstarch

2 tablespoons light brown sugar

¼ teaspoon kosher salt

For the crumble topping

½ packed cup [100 g] light brown sugar

½ cup [70 g] whole wheat flour

½ cup [60 g] rolled oats

½ teaspoon kosher salt

½ teaspoon ground cinnamon

6 tablespoons unsalted butter, cut into small pieces, at room temperature

First, preheat your oven to 350°F [175°C].

Next, prepare the blueberries
Place the blueberries in a large bowl with the lemon juice, cornstarch, brown sugar, and salt. Mix well. Transfer the mixture to a 9-inch [23-cm] pie pan (or ovenproof skillet). No need to wash the bowl!

Then prepare the crumble topping
In the same bowl you mixed the blueberries in, stir together the brown sugar, whole wheat flour, oats, salt, and cinnamon. Add the butter and then work the mixture with your hands, rubbing it between

your fingertips, to form large crumbs. Really scrunch it with your hands so it's like dense, wet, moldable sand.

Assemble and bake
Dot the top of the blueberries evenly with the crumb mixture. Bake until the berries are bubbling and the crumbs are dark golden brown, about 45 minutes.

Allow the crumble to cool for at least 10 minutes before serving. Serve warm or at room temperature.

PUMPKIN + HONEY PIE

Sweetened with honey, made luscious with cream, and gently spiced, this pumpkin pie is what I always want pumpkin pie to be but rarely is. I use a simple graham cracker crust here because it's so much easier to make than regular pie crust, plus it adds a nice contrasting crust to the smooth filling. If you can't imagine pumpkin pie without regular pie crust, feel free to use an unbaked 9-inch [23-cm] pie crust (homemade or store-bought . . . and, by the way, no one will know the difference).

Makes one 9-inch [23-cm] pie, serves 8 to 10

For the crust

5 ounces [144 g] graham crackers (1 sleeve from a standard package)

1 teaspoon ground cinnamon

½ teaspoon kosher salt

6 tablespoons unsalted butter, melted

For the filling

2 large eggs

One 15-ounce [425 g] can pumpkin (not pie filling!)

½ cup [120 ml] heavy cream

⅔ cup [160 ml] honey

½ teaspoon kosher salt

1½ teaspoons ground ginger

¼ teaspoon ground cloves

For the topping

1 cup [240 ml] heavy cream

3 tablespoons honey

¼ teaspoon kosher salt

First, preheat your oven to 350°F [175°C].

Next, make the crust

Place the graham crackers in a food processor and blitz until finely ground (or place in a large plastic bag, and crush with a rolling pin until the crumbs are very fine). You should have 1½ cups of crumbs.

Transfer the crumbs to a large bowl and stir in the cinnamon and salt. Then stir in the melted butter.

Transfer the crumbs to a 9-inch [23-cm] pie pan and spread them out to cover the surface. Use the underside of a measuring cup to press the crumbs down firmly so they form a nice even layer on the bottom and sides of the pan.

Then make the filling

Place the eggs in a large bowl and whisk well to combine. Whisk in the pumpkin, heavy cream, honey, salt, ginger, and cloves. Transfer the filling to the prepared crust.

Bake and cool

Bake the pie until a paring knife inserted in the filling near the edge of the pie comes out clean and the whole pie still has a slight jiggle but none of the filling is loose, about 1 hour and 10 minutes.

Place the pie on a cookie cooling rack and allow it to cool to room temperature. Proceed with the topping or cover, refrigerate for up to 3 days, and then bring back to room temperature before topping and serving.

Last, make the topping and serve

Place the heavy cream, honey, and salt in a large bowl. Use an electric handheld mixer on high speed (or use an electric stand mixer or just a whisk and a lot of elbow grease) to allow the cream to form soft peaks (like a pillow of whipped cream). Spoon the cream on top of the pie. Cut into wedges and serve immediately.

ANY FROZEN FRUIT + CORNMEAL COBBLER

Not only is this cobbler the easiest dessert to make in this book, it's also one of the homiest and most comforting. You mix the frozen fruit right in the baking dish and mix the topping in a bowl, pour it over the fruit, and there you have it. It's also really flexible. I use half-and-half in the batter since it's what I put in my coffee every single morning, so it's always in my refrigerator, but you could swap it for half milk and half cream, or even half milk and half sour cream or yogurt. You can make this all frozen peaches, all frozen cherries, or all frozen berries, or a mix of whatever similar fruit you'd like. While you can use fresh fruit when it's in season (you want about 2 pounds [907 g] total and need to pit whatever needs pitting and peel whatever needs peeling), the convenience and consistency of frozen fruit is not to be underestimated. Whatever you do, don't skip the vanilla ice cream! The cobbler is purposely not very sweet, and the vanilla ice cream really brings it all home. Leftovers can be wrapped in plastic and refrigerated for up to a few days and rewarmed in a 300°F [150°C] oven until warm. Pro tip: it's great cold for breakfast with yogurt!

Serves 8

For the fruit filling

2 pounds [907 g] frozen fruit (for this photo, I did my favorite—a mix of peaches, cherries, and raspberries—but use whatever you like)

2 tablespoons fresh lemon juice

2 tablespoons cornstarch

2 tablespoons granulated sugar

For the cobbler topping

¾ cup [98 g] yellow cornmeal

¾ cup [94 g] all-purpose flour

½ cup [100 g] granulated sugar

2 teaspoons baking powder

½ teaspoon kosher salt

1 cup [240 ml] half-and-half

3 tablespoons unsalted butter, melted

To serve

Vanilla ice cream

First, preheat your oven to 375°F [190°C].

Next, prepare the fruit filling
Place the frozen fruit, lemon juice, cornstarch, and sugar in a 9-by-13-inch [23-by-33-cm] baking dish and mix well with your hands to combine.

Then make the cobbler topping
Place cornmeal, flour, sugar, baking powder, and salt in a large bowl and whisk well to combine. Stir in the half-and-half and melted butter.

Evenly pour the batter over the fruit.

And bake
Bake the cobbler until the topping is dark golden brown and the fruit is bubbling, about 45 minutes.

Let the cobbler sit for at least 15 minutes before serving to allow the juices to settle. Serve warm or at room temperature with vanilla ice cream.

COCONUT MARBLE LOAF

My grandparents ran Ratchick's, a classic Ashkenazi Jewish bakery on Avenue J and 15th Street in Brooklyn, for decades. It closed before I was born and while I never got to go to it, I feel like it's a part of me. It sometimes feels like I miss something I never actually had, a blurry longing that my mother, who is a first-generation American, says is very familiar to her. The most evocative way I know to weave my family legacy with the present is to learn about the things my grandfather baked, the items their customers purchased. Food helps bridge not only communities, but also generations.

When I've talked to my family about their favorite things from the bakery, two items stand out: marble rye bread (a swirl of pumpernickel dough mixed with rye dough) and marble loaf cake, chocolate and vanilla pound cake batters layered and baked together.

On theme, I set out to make a marble loaf that was a little old, but also a little unexpected. Something tied to my past, but also tied to me. And I adore coconut. So here it is, a tender loaf cake made rich with coconut milk and coconut flour (if you can't find it, use ¼ cup each cornstarch and all-purpose flour). Feel free to add a handful of chocolate chips to the chocolate batter for a little extra chocolate oomph if you'd like.

Makes 1 loaf (serves about 8)

Cooking spray (my preference is olive oil spray, but use whatever you have)

2 large eggs

1 cup [240 ml] canned coconut milk (shake before measuring; if separated, blend before measuring)

½ cup [120 ml] canola oil (or other neutral oil such as vegetable)

1 cup [200 g] granulated sugar

¼ teaspoon coconut extract (or almond extract)

1½ cups [188 g] all-purpose flour

½ cup [56 g] coconut flour

2 teaspoons baking powder

1 teaspoon kosher salt

½ cup [85 g/3 ounces] dark or semisweet chocolate chips, melted (see instructions on page 227 for more direction on melting chocolate)

Preheat your oven to 350°F [175°C].

Coat a 9-by-5-inch [23-by-12-cm] loaf pan with cooking spray.

Place the eggs in a large bowl and whisk well to combine. Add the coconut milk, canola oil, sugar, and coconut extract and whisk well to combine.

In a separate bowl, whisk together the flours, baking powder, and salt.

Stir the dry ingredients into the wet ingredients (hang onto the bowl you had the dry ingredients in). Transfer half of the batter into the now-empty flour bowl. Stir the melted chocolate into one of the batter bowls. Two batters for the price of one!

Use two spoons to put alternating scoops of the plain and the chocolate batters in the loaf pan. Depending on the size of your scoops (each about two tablespoons), you'll probably end up doing two layers of scoops. Don't stress about this; it's not an exam, it's just a loaf cake.

Bake the cake until a toothpick tests clean and no batter jiggles when you give the loaf a little shake, about 1 hour and 5 minutes.

Let the loaf cool, preferably on a wire rack to speed up cooling, until it reaches room temperature, then remove it from its pan. Cut into thick slices and serve.

LEMON RICOTTA CUPCAKES

A nod to the lemon ricotta pancakes Grace used to love at Five Leaves, a restaurant near our old apartment in Brooklyn, these cupcakes are so easy to make and feel so happy. You can prepare them, frosted, up to a day ahead. Just refrigerate them and bring back to room temperature before serving. If you don't have a food processor, you can make the frosting by hand with an electric handheld mixer or just a whisk and a lot of elbow grease. The food processor is the best tool for the job, though, because it really combines the ricotta and cream cheese together in the smoothest, airiest way.

Makes 1 dozen

For the cupcakes

1 cup [125 g] all-purpose flour

½ cup [55 g] almond flour (or just additional all-purpose flour)

½ cup [100 g] granulated sugar

2 teaspoons baking powder

½ teaspoon kosher salt

2 large eggs

1 cup [235 g] whole milk ricotta cheese

Finely grated zest and juice of 1 large lemon

½ cup [1 stick, aka 8 tablespoons, aka 113 g] unsalted butter, melted

For the frosting

½ cup [118 g] whole milk ricotta cheese

½ cup [4 ounces, aka 113 g] cream cheese, at room temperature

¼ cup [30 g] powdered sugar

Finely grated zest of 1 large lemon (reserve the lemon if you'd like to use it for garnish)

¼ teaspoon kosher salt

First, make the cupcakes
Preheat your oven to 350°F [175°C]. Line a 12-compartment standard muffin tin with paper liners.

Place the flours, sugar, baking powder, and salt in a large bowl and whisk well to combine.

Place the eggs in a large bowl and whisk well. Whisk in the ricotta, lemon zest and lemon juice, and the melted butter. Stir the dry mixture into the wet mixture until just combined.

Evenly divide the batter among the cups in the lined muffin tin (the batter will fill the cups). Bake the cupcakes until firm to the touch and a toothpick tests clean, about 25 minutes.

Transfer the cupcakes to a wire rack, and cool to room temperature before frosting.

Then make the frosting
Place the ricotta, cream cheese, powdered sugar, lemon zest, and salt in the bowl of a food processor and blitz until smooth and slightly whipped, about 2 minutes of processing (pause once or twice to scrape down the sides of the bowl).

And serve
Evenly divide the frosting among the cooled cupcakes. You can pipe it, spoon it, spatula it . . . just get it on there! If you'd like, thinly slice the lemon you zested for the frosting and put a slice on each cupcake for garnish. This is not only pretty, it also lets people know to expect lemon.

Serve the cupcakes at room temperature.

PEAR, POLENTA + ALMOND CAKE

The L Word, the Showtime television series that ran for six seasons, was all about a group of queer women in Los Angeles. While it was far from a perfect show, it definitely played a big role in my life when I watched it in college and was figuring out a lot about my own identity. What does this have to do with this cake? One of the characters, Kit Porter (played by the great Pam Grier), runs The Planet, basically the Central Perk of *The L Word*, the café where the group hangs out all the time. More than once she mentions that The Planet's pear polenta tart is the café's best-seller. I've had this tart on my mind for over a decade. How did they make it? What did it taste like? And after years of tweaking, I ended up making it into . . . a simple cake. I just think it's so much easier to make than a tart. Also, this cake is gluten-free, which feels very Los Angeles to me. Note that I call for some pear baby food in the batter. This might seem like a strange item to go into a cake, but it's way easier than making your own pureed pear and it adds pear flavor, plus essential moisture, to the batter (you could substitute applesauce). Last, if you only have an 9-inch [23-cm] cake pan, don't worry. Use it and just decrease the baking time by 10 minutes.

Serves 8 to 10

For the cake

Cooking spray (my preference is olive oil spray, but use whatever you have)

1½ cups [195 g] yellow cornmeal

1½ cups [165 g] almond flour

2 teaspoons baking powder

½ teaspoon salt

2 large eggs

¾ cup [180 ml] olive oil

Two 4-ounce [113 g] jars pear baby food

½ teaspoon almond extract (or ¼ teaspoon if you just want a whisper, or none if you don't like almond extract)

½ cup [100 g] granulated sugar

For the topping

1 large firm pear (any type), cored and cut into ¼-inch [½-cm] slices (no need to peel)

3 tablespoons blanched sliced almonds

For serving

Powdered sugar (optional)

First, preheat your oven to 350°F [175°C].

Spray an 8-inch [20-cm] cake pan with cooking spray and set it aside. To make the cake easier to remove later, cut a piece of parchment into a long strip measuring roughly 2 inches [5 cm] wide and 12 inches [30 cm] long. Press it on the bottom of the pan, coat it with a quick spritz of cooking spray, and

let the excess stick up so once you pour the batter into the pan and bake it, you'll have two little handles to help you lift the cooled cake out later.

Next, make the cake batter
Place the cornmeal, almond flour, baking powder, and salt in a medium bowl and whisk well to combine.

(continued)

Place the eggs in another large bowl and whisk well. Whisk in the olive oil, pear baby food, almond extract, and sugar.

Stir the dry mixture into the wet mixture and then transfer the batter to the prepared pan and use a spoon to spread it out so that it's in an even layer.

Then top the cake
Fan the pear slices on top of the batter in a nice pattern, but don't stress about it—it doesn't have to be perfect—just make sure the slices are in an even layer so that they bake evenly (it's okay if they overlap a bit).

Evenly sprinkle the sliced almonds on top.

And bake
Bake until exposed cake bits are dark golden brown and the whole thing looks delicious and a toothpick tests clean (poke it between the pear slices so it doesn't get soggy), about 1 hour and 10 minutes.

Let the cake cool to room temperature, preferably on a wire rack to speed up cooling, and then use those little parchment handles to lift it out and transfer it to a serving dish. Dust lightly with powdered sugar (if using), cut into wedges, and serve at room temperature. Seriously, wait for it to cool. It will crumble too much if you try to slice it while it's warm. Leftovers keep well wrapped in plastic at room temperature for up to a few days.

BANANA + CHOCOLATE CHIP LAYER CAKE

CARROT PINEAPPLE CAKE WITH
MAPLE CREAM CHEESE FROSTING

CARROT PINEAPPLE CAKE WITH MAPLE CREAM CHEESE FROSTING

During college I spent so much time at the Hungarian Pastry Shop, a café in Morningside Heights in Manhattan. I was an English major with a concentration in creative writing and wanted so much to *feel* like a real writer. For me, that feeling came when I sat at the pastry shop in a dark corner with lots of coffee, a notebook, and a piece of carrot cake, writing extremely earnest poetry. Surrounded by other writers with their cookies and cakes and mugs, my time at the Hungarian Pastry Shop made me feel like I might actually be able to call myself a writer. Flash forward to today, I now get to sit at home with bottomless pots of coffee and write recipes and stories like this one. And these days I make my own cake.

This carrot cake is like a cross between a traditional carrot cake and a hummingbird cake, the banana-pineapple cake from the American South. The pineapple adds so much sweetness and moisture, which allows you to get away with a bit less sugar (most cakes call for a couple of cups, but here we can get away with just one and it's still plenty sweet). The almond flour in the batter helps to make the cake really tender (plus it lowers the overall amount of carbohydrates if that's something you pay attention to). You can always just substitute all-purpose flour in its place. If you'd prefer cupcakes, you'll get 18 standard ones from this batter (bake in lined muffin tins until a toothpick tests clean, about 22 minutes, and then frost).

Serves 8 to 10

For the cake

Cooking spray (my preference is olive oil spray, but use whatever you have)

1½ cups [188 g] all-purpose flour

1 cup [110 g] almond flour

1 cup [200 g] granulated sugar

2 teaspoons baking soda

1 teaspoon baking powder

1 teaspoon kosher salt

1 teaspoon ground cinnamon

1 teaspoon ground ginger

One 8-ounce [227 g] can crushed pineapple in pineapple juice

3 large eggs, lightly beaten

1 cup [240 ml] canola oil (or other neutral oil such as vegetable)

½ pound [227 g] carrots, peeled and coarsely grated (about 3 medium carrots, or 2 loosely packed cups grated carrots)

For the frosting

1½ cups [12 ounces, aka 340 g] cream cheese, at room temperature

¼ cup [56 g] sour cream

¼ cup [60 ml] maple syrup

¼ teaspoon kosher salt

First, make the cake
Preheat your oven to 350°F [175°C]. Spray two 8-inch [20-cm] cake pans with cooking spray and set them aside.

Place the flours in a medium bowl with the sugar, baking soda, baking powder, salt, cinnamon, and ginger and whisk well to combine. Give it a few extra whisks just to guarantee everything is combined evenly. Add the crushed pineapple along with its juice, the eggs, and the oil and stir well to combine. Stir in the carrots. Divide the batter between the 2 cake pans and use a spoon to spread the tops of each to make sure they're nice and even.

Bake the cakes until firm to the touch and a toothpick tests clean, about 40 minutes. If the cakes aren't on the same rack in the oven, rotate them halfway through baking.

Let the cakes cool completely to room temperature, preferably on a wire rack to speed up cooling, before frosting.

Then make the frosting
Place the cream cheese, sour cream, maple syrup, and salt in a large bowl. Use an electric handheld mixer (or use an electric stand mixer or just a whisk and a lot of elbow grease) to mix everything together until light and fluffy, about 1 minute. It's best to do this while the cakes are in the oven and then refrigerate the frosting while the cakes bake and then cool. This gives the frosting a chance to get a bit firmer. It's totally fine if you do it last minute, though.

And serve
Remove each cake from its pan. Place one cake on a serving platter or cake stand (whatever you will serve it on) and spread half of the frosting evenly over it. Place the second cake on top and coat the sides and top of the cake with the remaining frosting (a small offset spatula is the best tool for the job, but a dinner knife works well, too). Don't worry about making this too perfect. Rustic is real and real is beautiful (put that in a skincare ad!).

Cut into wedges and serve at room temperature. Leftovers can be wrapped in plastic wrap and stored in the refrigerator for up to 3 days (bring the cake back to room temperature before serving).

BANANA + CHOCOLATE CHIP LAYER CAKE

As simple to make as a loaf of banana bread, but way more exciting, this cake makes for an excellent birthday cake or holiday dessert. Some notes. First, this is the perfect place for your overripe bananas, and I actually keep a stash in our freezer and then take them out an hour or so before making the batter (freezing them makes them even more soft and mushy and perfect for baking). Second, you can make the cake layers ahead and then frost before serving, or you can refrigerate the frosted cake for up to a day or two—it's quite good served cold. Third, if you only own a single cake pan, fear not! Simply pour the batter into the pan and bake until a toothpick tests clean (it will take about 15 minutes longer in the oven than the two separate layers; and once the cake cools completely, use a serrated knife to cut it into two layers). And, last, you can absolutely turn this cake into cupcakes (you'll get 18) by baking the batter in lined muffin tins (they will take about 20 to 25 minutes to bake) and then frosting.

Serves 8 to 10

For the cake

Cooking spray (my preference is olive oil spray, but use whatever you have)

1 cup [125 g] all-purpose flour

1 cup [140 g] whole wheat flour

1 cup [200 g] granulated sugar

2 teaspoons baking powder

1 teaspoon baking soda

1 teaspoon kosher salt

4 extremely ripe bananas, peeled

2 large eggs

1 cup [227 g] sour cream

½ cup [120 ml] canola oil (or other neutral oil such as vegetable)

6 ounces [170 g] semisweet chocolate chips (about 1 cup)

For the frosting

6 ounces [170 g] semisweet chocolate chips (about 1 cup)

1 cup [227 g] sour cream, at room temperature

1 tablespoon maple syrup

First, make the cake

Preheat your oven to 350°F [175°C]. Spray two 8-inch [20-cm] cake pans with cooking spray and set them aside.

Place the flours, sugar, baking powder, baking soda, and salt in a medium bowl and whisk well to combine.

Place the bananas in a large bowl and use a fork or potato masher to mash them well and make a banana puree (it's okay if it's not totally smooth). Add the eggs, sour cream, and canola oil and whisk well to combine. Stir the dry ingredients into the wet ingredients and then fold in the chocolate chips.

Evenly divide the batter between the cake pans and use a spoon to spread the tops of both to form even layers.

Bake the cakes until golden brown, firm to the touch, and a toothpick tests clean, about 35 minutes.

Let the cakes cool to room temperature, preferably on a wire rack to speed up cooling.

Then make the frosting
(make it while the layers bake!)
Place the chocolate chips in a microwave-safe bowl and microwave in 15-second bursts, stirring in between each, until the chocolate is melted. Depending on the strength of your microwave, it will probably take 3 or 4 rounds of this. Don't skip the stirring in between microwave bursts. Chocolate melts before it looks like it fully does and you don't want to burn it. If you don't have a microwave, put the chocolate in a metal or glass bowl over a small pot of simmering water (don't let it touch the water) and stir until melted.

Add the sour cream and maple syrup to the melted chocolate and whisk until smooth. Refrigerate the frosting until you're ready to use it (it will thicken as it cools and be even easier to use). This, in and of itself, is the easiest ever chocolate mousse (I won't tell if you sneak a bite!).

And serve
Remove each cooled cake from its pan. Place one cake on a serving platter or cake stand (whatever you will serve it on) and spread half of the frosting evenly over it. Place the second cake on top and coat the sides and top of the cake with the remaining frosting (a small offset spatula is the best tool for the job, but a dinner knife works well, too). Don't stress about making this perfect. The more real, the better. Serve immediately or refrigerate for up to a day or two before serving (it's good cold!).

CREAM CHEESE
PARM

LEMONS
AVO x 2
CUKES!

KETCHUP
BLACK BEANS
WW FLOUR
AP FLOUR

SEVEN LISTS

Ranging from thoughts for what to do with leftover buttermilk to tips for keeping your kitchen organized, each of these Seven Lists contains seven ideas I couldn't resist sharing with you. I hope they help make your life in, and adjacent to, your kitchen a little easier.

SEVEN THINGS I LEARNED FROM BEING A PRIVATE CHEF

1. **KEEP YOUR PANTRY STOCKED.** This might sound like a cliché, but it really makes a dent in the ready-for-anything category. And while we all might dream of someone from HGTV making us a walk-in situation with floating shelves and rows of identical containers, I think it's worth pointing out that a pantry can be one deep drawer or a single shelf. Filling it doesn't have to be stressful. When you buy a can of chickpeas for a recipe, buy an extra. Same goes for a box of pasta, a bottle of olive oil, a bag of rice, canned tomatoes, and so on. This all means on a day when you have less time than you hoped (every day, am I right?), your kitchen has your back. When I was a private chef, there was always "one more person joining us," and having those extra essentials meant I could always stretch a meal with ease, plus I could skip a trip to the store.

2. **IF TIME PERMITS, SHOP THE DAY BEFORE A BIG COOK (LIKE BEFORE A PARTY OR A HOLIDAY).** It's its own big job. And write your grocery list by section (dairy, produce, dry goods, etc.). Put everything away and then put your feet up. You'll cook tomorrow.

3. **ALWAYS THINK OF YOUR FUTURE SELF. IF YOU'RE ROASTING A CHICKEN, ROAST TWO.** If you're making cookie dough, double the batch. Same goes for a pot of soup, a tray of meatballs, or a blender full of salad dressing. You're already gathering the ingredients for all these things and doing the motions, so go ahead and do your future self a favor. Portioned, frozen cookie dough means you can pop just a couple in the oven at any moment (or your toaster oven, let's be real). An extra chicken means for the next few days you'll have what you need for spontaneous chicken tacos, sandwiches, or salads. A container of frozen soup or chili means you have something on hand for unexpected guests (or something to bring to a friend in need, and yes, sometimes that friend is yourself).

4. **DISCLAIMERS DON'T TASTE GOOD.** If something didn't turn out how you planned it, there's no need to tell your guests what the original plan was. Just say "dinner's ready!" You made someone a meal! That is a gift.

5. **DON'T UNDERESTIMATE THE VALUE OF A HOMEY DESSERT.** Even when I cooked for very fancy people, I never made fancy desserts. And do you know what? I think that's part of what kept me employed. Whether I served a cobbler, a simple cake, or ice cream sundaes, my clients ended their meals feeling comforted and happy. Isn't that how we'd all like to feel?

ERIN + SAM (LONG SEASON FARM), 2020

6. SUPPORT THE PEOPLE WHO GROW, GATHER, SOURCE, AND SELL YOUR FOOD. The best part of being a private chef was getting to spend other people's money on really good ingredients. When I'm spending my own money, I'm even more discerning about who I am supporting. And in doing so, I feel more connected to so much of the food I eat. Whether you shop at a farmers' market, join a CSA, or order your holiday pies and cakes from a local bakery, connecting the dots helps to make the food system, and the world, a little smaller.

7. SPEAKING OF SPENDING OTHER PEOPLES' MONEY, I got to see a lot of extreme wealth up close when I worked as a private chef. Cooking in my various clients' kitchens over the years really showed me that while money can buy you all the lobster you want and makes lots of things easier, it doesn't actually make life free from pain or challenges. My biggest gift from those years has been to reassess how I measure wealth and to learn that community is the currency I most want to invest in.

SEVEN KITCHEN ORGANIZATION TIPS

1. **WHETHER YOU'RE A SPRING CLEANER, A NEW YEAR'S DAY RESOLVER, OR JUST HAVE A RANDOM SUNDAY WITH NOTHING TO DO, TAKE A DAY ONCE A YEAR TO TAKE EVERYTHING OUT OF YOUR REFRIGERATOR, KITCHEN CABINETS, AND DRAWERS.** Wipe down the shelves and surfaces. Throw away or compost anything that's gone bad or dried up or anything like that (and get rid of any broken tools). Make a donation pile for anything that's still good (and sealed) that you haven't used in over a year (this goes for tools, too). If a whole year has gone by and you haven't used it, you probably won't any time soon. Bring that box to your local food pantry or see if a neighbor or friend might want something. Then put everything that remains away. But put it away with consideration. Don't be afraid to adjust your adjustable shelves. Make your everyday things accessible.

2. **GO THROUGH ALL YOUR CONTAINERS AND MAKE SURE YOU HAVE MATCHING LIDS.** Any containers without lids can be used in drawers to hold small things like measuring spoons or stamps in your miscellaneous drawer (we all have one), but otherwise they need to go (same goes for lids that have no matching containers). They're just taking up space. Recycle whatever can be recycled.

3. **EMBRACE TURNTABLES IN YOUR CUPBOARDS AND REFRIGERATOR!** They're game-changers because they allow you to just spin the whole thing and see everything. No more forgetting about the bottles in the back. No more buying multiples of the same thing because you forgot you already have it on hand. You can get small turntables from places like the Container Store (I personally swear by the ones made by OXO since they "grip" the surface they sit on). Get as many as you can fit in your kitchen and use them for everything (and by "everything" I mean vinegars, oils, soy sauce, vitamins, jam, jars of pickles and olives, and more).

4. **PUT LIKE WITH LIKE.** Meaning, all of your vinegars should be together, all of your nuts in another place, your grains in another. Pretend your pantry is your own private, curated grocery store. You want to be able to find everything. Don't make a system that you have to fit your items into, make a system that works for your items.

5. **IF YOU HAVE A DRAWER TO SPARE, PUT YOUR SPICES THERE.** Not only are drawers dark when they're closed (good for spices!), it also means you can look at your entire spice collection at once instead of just the first row inside of an overcrowded cabinet. Label the tops of all your spices if they aren't labeled already (a permanent marker on a white cap works, or just affix a little piece of masking tape and then write the name of the spice on that).

6. **LABEL EVERYTHING WHERE YOU CAN SEE IT.** If you can't see the top of a container when it's sitting on a shelf in your refrigerator, label the side. Keep a roll of masking tape and a Sharpie wherever you store your containers so that when you put leftovers away, you automatically remember to label them.

7. **FOLLOWING A BIG KITCHEN ORGANIZATION, GIVE YOURSELF SOME FLEXIBILITY.** After a week or so, you might find that you wish you had put your canned beans in a different place or that your oils were on a lower shelf. It's your kitchen! Feel free to move things around. Make your kitchen work for you.

SEVEN MEANINGFUL CONVERSATION PROMPTS

One of my mom's favorite stories to share is that her kindergarten teacher would give a single gold star for a correct answer, but two gold stars for a good question. I love a good question. It opens the world up. I spend a lot of time thinking about questions and how to phrase them, especially when it comes to preparing to interview people for my podcast or when I moderate panel discussions. A good conversation, one that feels meaningful and connected, stems from the questions we ask each other and the ability to be present when we offer and listen to answers. Here are some of my favorite questions to spark conversation around your kitchen table since the best thing about any meal isn't the food, it's the connection that comes when we've eaten well and can relax into each other's company. These are also handy for long car rides or phone calls with friends or family members that you're missing.

1. What was your favorite thing to eat growing up? Did you request something special for your birthday?

2. When was the last time someone surprised you with a random act of kindness? And when was the last time you surprised someone with one?

3. What's the most meaningful gift you've ever received? And the most meaningful one you've given?

4. What do you see when you close your eyes and picture your "happy place"?

5. What's the most recent finish line you crossed?

6. If you were in charge of a large sum of money for your community, how would you distribute it?

7. Who is someone you'd like to write a thank-you note to? What would you say?

SEVEN WAYS TO USE LEFTOVER EGG WHITES OR EGG YOLKS

1. **GRANOLA:** Lightly whipped egg whites help make granola crunchy. For a very basic granola, mix together 3 cups [360 g] rolled oats with ¼ cup [60 ml] *each* extra-virgin olive oil and maple syrup, plus 1 teaspoon kosher salt. Whip 2 egg whites together until very frothy and then stir them into the oat mixture. Spread out in an even layer on a parchment-lined sheet pan. Bake in a 400°F [200°C] oven, stirring every 10 minutes, until browned, about 30 minutes. Let it cool to room temperature (it will crisp as it cools). Feel free to jazz up this basic recipe with different grains, nuts, or spices. Also feel free to mix in any type of dried fruit after the granola is baked. For example, for almond-cherry granola, add a few drops of almond extract to the egg whites, put lots of crunchy almonds in the oat mixture, and stir together with dried cherries after baking. For a garam masala, pistachio, and apricot granola, add garam masala and pistachios to the oats and fold in chopped dried apricots after baking. And so on. Store granola in a container at room temperature. Technically it lasts a while, but I find it hard to keep around very long.

2. **SPICED NUTS:** Just like with the granola, lightly whipped egg whites help keep roasted nuts crisp and also give you a way of making spices stick well to nuts before roasting them. To make them, whisk together 2 egg whites until frothy. Add 1 pound (about 4 cups) raw nuts. This could be all cashews or almonds or whatever, or a mix of nuts. Then add 1 tablespoon kosher salt, 2 tablespoons of granulated sugar, and 2 tablespoons whatever spices you like (for example, Old Bay, or equal parts turmeric and cumin, or equal parts cinnamon and ginger with a whisper of cayenne). Mix well and spread out on a parchment-lined sheet pan. Bake in a 300°F [150°C] oven, stirring every 15 minutes, until very browned, about 45 minutes. Let the nuts cool (they will crisp as they cool). Store in a container at room temperature.

3. **COCONUT MACAROONS:** Whipped egg whites help bind coconut and sweetened condensed milk together for these favorite gluten-free cookies (they're wonderful for Passover). For 20 cookies, mix together a 14-ounce [397 g] bag of sweetened, shredded coconut with a 14-ounce [397 g] can sweetened condensed milk. Whisk 2 egg whites together with 1 teaspoon each vanilla extract and kosher salt until they form stiff peaks (you can use a handheld electric mixer or an electric stand mixer, too). Fold the egg whites into the coconut mixture. Drop spoonfuls of the mixture onto a parchment-lined sheet pan and bake in a 325°F [160°C] oven until golden, about 30 minutes. Let cool before serving.

4. MINIATURE EGG WHITE FRITTATAS: For each egg white you have, you'll make one frittata. Coat the cups of a standard muffin tray generously with cooking spray (just spray as many as you'll use to make frittatas). Fill each cup two-thirds full with whatever fillings you'd like (cheese, cooked vegetables, crumbled cooked sausage or bacon, herbs, etc.). Lightly whisk your egg whites together until they're a little frothy and season with salt and pepper and then evenly divide among the muffin cups. Bake in a 300°F [150°C] oven until the frittatas are puffed and firm, about 20 minutes. They will deflate a little as they cool. Serve warm or at room temperature. These are great to make on a Sunday so you have a grab-and-go breakfast for the week! They're also a great snack.

5. BLENDER HOLLANDAISE: A great place for egg yolks, hollandaise sauce is a best friend to eggs Benedict, steamed asparagus, and broiled fish. While it might seem intimidating, I find using the blender method to be pretty foolproof. Melt a stick of butter [113 g] and keep it nearby. In a blender, whiz together 3 egg yolks, 1 tablespoon lemon juice, and ½ teaspoon salt until thickened, about 30 seconds. If your blender has speeds, turn yours down to low (if not, don't worry). While the machine is running, slowly stream in the melted butter to form a thick, emulsified sauce. Season to taste with more lemon and salt as needed. Serve immediately while still warm.

6. KEY LIME PIE: Egg yolks are essential for key lime pie, one of the world's best desserts. For one pie, whisk together a 14-ounce [397 g] can sweetened condensed milk together with 3 egg yolks and ½ cup [120 ml] key lime juice (I use Nellie & Joe's, available in most grocery stores). Pour the mixture into a 9-inch [23-cm] graham cracker crust (store-bought or homemade, like the one on page 213). Bake in a 350°F [175°C] oven for 20 minutes and then let cool to room temperature and refrigerate until chilled and firm, at least 2 hours and up to 3 days. Top with whipped cream before serving if you'd like (I like`˙.˙.`).

7. LEMON CURD: When life gives you lemons`˙.˙.` and egg yolks`˙.˙.` make lemon curd. To make 1½ cups [360 ml], place 4 egg yolks, ½ cup [100 g] granulated sugar, the finely grated zest of 1 lemon, and the juice of 2 lemons into a heat-safe bowl and whisk together over a saucepan of simmering water until the mixture is noticeably thickened, a full 10 minutes. Take the bowl off the heat and whisk in 4 tablespoons softened butter, 1 tablespoon at a time. Transfer it to a container and let cool to room temperature. Cover and refrigerate for at least 2 hours, and up to 3 days, before serving. Spoon on your next scone or slice of toasted, buttered brioche. Use it to fill a tart or to top ice cream, pancakes, or waffles. Use it to fill crepes or a layer cake. Use it in a trifle. Fold it together with equal parts whipped cream to make lemon mousse. Or just eat it by the spoonful!

SEVEN WAYS TO USE LEFTOVER BUTTERMILK

1. BUTTERMILK + HONEY PUDDING: For 6 servings, sprinkle 1½ teaspoons unflavored gelatin (available in the baking aisle) into a small bowl with 2 tablespoons room temperature water. Let it sit until it softens, about 10 minutes. Place ¾ cup [180 ml] heavy cream in a small saucepan with ¼ cup [60 ml] honey and a pinch of salt and heat just until bubbles form around the edge. Turn off the heat, whisk in the softened gelatin, and let the mixture cool until it's just lukewarm. Whisk in 2 cups [480 ml] buttermilk and then divide the mixture among 6 small cups or bowls and refrigerate until set, about 2 hours. You can keep these in the fridge for up to a couple of days. Very nice served with fresh berries or a spoonful of jam.

2. BUTTERMILK SOFT SERVE: Whisk honey or maple syrup into your buttermilk so it's as sweet as you like it (start with a little, as it's easier to add than take out). Add a pinch of salt, too. Then throw it in your ice cream maker and let the machine do all the heavy lifting. The only catch is this really needs to be enjoyed immediately while it's smooth and creamy, straight from the machine. Freezing it, like you would for regular homemade ice cream, leaves you with a solid block of frozen buttermilk. Not the worst thing in the world, but not soft serve. So make this right before you want to eat it!

3. GRACE'S FAVORITE BISCUITS: For light, fluffy, EASY biscuits, whisk together 2 cups [250 g] all-purpose flour with 1 tablespoon baking powder and 1 teaspoon kosher salt. Stir in 1 cup [240 ml] buttermilk to form a shaggy dough. If it's too dry, add more buttermilk 1 tablespoon at a time (same goes with flour if the dough is too wet). Lightly flour your work surface and shape the dough into a 6-inch [15-cm] round and then use a chef's knife to cut into 6 wedges. Space them out on a parchment-lined sheet pan, brush with a little more buttermilk, and bake in a 425°F [220°C] oven until golden brown, 15 to 20 minutes. Serve hot with butter and honey.

4. BUTTERMILK + CORNMEAL PANCAKES: For 4 servings, whisk together 1 cup [125 g] all-purpose flour, 1 cup [140 g] yellow cornmeal, 2 tablespoons granulated sugar, 2 teaspoons baking powder, and 1 teaspoon salt. Whisk in 2 large eggs and 2 cups [480 ml] buttermilk. Cook in a hot buttered skillet in small rounds, adjusting the heat as needed, until cooked through and browned on both sides. Serve with even more butter, maple syrup or honey, and a pinch of salt.

5. BUTTERMILK CHICKEN: Buttermilk and chicken have always been very good friends, and the best thing to do with leftover buttermilk is to marinate chicken in it before roasting, a technique popularized by the one and only Samin Nosrat (hi, SN!). Whether you do a whole chicken or just parts (like a bunch of chicken legs or wings or even a bunch of boneless, skinless chicken breasts), season buttermilk with salt and that's that, or add other spices like paprika and garlic powder or cumin and turmeric, and then pour it into a resealable bag with the chicken and make sure it's all coated. Marinate in the refrigerator for at least 1 hour and up to 24 hours. Roast in a skillet or on a sheet pan in a 400°F [200°C] oven until the chicken is cooked through (the time depends on what type of chicken you're cooking).

6. MASHED POTATOES: Classic for a reason, buttermilk mashed potatoes are one of the most comforting places to put leftover buttermilk. Just boil some peeled and diced potatoes (I love Yukon Golds since they're so buttery), drain well, and mash with enough buttermilk (and melted butter, too, because life is short) until they're the consistency you like. Season with plenty of salt.

7. SMOOTHIES: Try buttermilk in your next smoothie instead of whatever type of liquid you typically use. I really like a combination of frozen bananas, frozen kale or spinach, buttermilk, and a tiny pinch of salt.

SEVEN TIPS FOR ACCOMMODATING DIETARY RESTRICTIONS

1. ASK AHEAD. Whenever I invite someone over, I always ask if they have any restrictions or anything else I should know about. Knowing ahead of time is much easier than trying to finagle something last minute. On a similar note, if you have an allergy or restriction, let your hosts know ahead of time.

2. KEEP IT SIMPLE AND KEEP IT SEPARATE. The more extensive my guests' dietary needs are, the more straightforward my cooking. A platter of roasted squash, a pot of rice, a roast chicken, and a chopped cucumber and chickpea salad is a meal that vegans, low-carb carnivores, and gluten-free'ers can all enjoy through mixing-and-matching. Better to have a few simple dishes rather than one complicated dish that many can't partake in.

3. SIMPLE DOES NOT NEED TO BE BORING. I've noticed that the people in my life who have a lot of dietary limitations usually end up eating the same foods over and over again. So I like to stick with what they can eat, but dial in on whatever I can do to make it more exciting. Let's take that meal I just described. Maybe I'll drizzle the roasted squash with some really good balsamic vinegar and sprinkle a few toasted hazelnuts on top. Maybe I'll stir some extra-virgin olive oil and chopped fresh herbs into the rice after it cooks. That chopped salad can be easily riffed on. Big chunks of juicy tomatoes and crisp cucumbers with a fresh oregano dressing, or maybe wedges of radicchio with a caper vinaigrette. All of these tweaks keep all of the dishes vegan and gluten-free and also keep them exciting. When you can't eat a lot of things, it's great to feel like you want to eat everything that's available.

4. INCLUDE, DON'T ALIENATE. Cooking in this simple-but-not-boring way, and keeping dishes separate so folks can mix-and-match, means that no one is an exception. There's no separate meal for the vegans. Everyone is included.

5. INFORM! Make sure everyone knows what's in everything. This can be done through a little announcement (tap your glass and say "Hey, everyone! I just want to run through what's for dinner!") or make little signs to put in front of dishes (this is a good task to assign to a young person in attendance).

6. DON'T FEAR DESSERT. Dessert can often be the hardest part of the meal to make work for everyone since it often involves a lot of the items that people avoid for whatever reason (including, but not limited to, dairy, wheat, and sugar). And you usually just serve one thing for dessert. But when you have a lot of restrictions to accommodate, apply the mix-and-match method to dessert, too. Serve a pan of roasted apples coated with a little olive oil, fresh ginger, and ground cinnamon (no gluten, dairy, or sugar), plus some unsweetened whipped cream (low-carb!) and a container of vegan ice cream (there are so many to choose from). Maybe put some roasted nuts on the table and a plate of cookies, too. Everyone can mix-and-match and be so happy.

7. DON'T BE AFRAID TO ASK FOR HELP. Having someone over is such a lovely thing to do and you don't need to make everything yourself to extend that invitation. Ask your guests to bring a dish they love so you are sure they'll have something they are sure to enjoy, plus you might learn about a new dish along the way.

SEVEN FAVORITE SOLO MEALS

1. **COLD BLUE CHEESE SALAD WITH HOT GRILLED STEAK:** The two foods Grace really doesn't like are blue cheese and steak, so I usually only eat them when she's away. I buy a small steak and take it out of the fridge an hour or so before I'm going to cook it so that it doesn't go from super cold to super hot. I cut a handful of cherry tomatoes in half or dice a big juicy tomato and put it in the bottom of a salad bowl with some thinly sliced red onion. I splash those with red wine vinegar and olive oil and season them generously with salt and let them just sit in that bath while I do everything else. I season the steak generously with salt and pepper and then get my grill going. When it's ripping hot, I grill it just until it's barely firm to the touch, maybe 2 or 3 minutes per side depending on how thick it is. I transfer it to a plate. While it sits and collects itself, I chop some iceberg or romaine lettuce and toss it with the tomato and onion mixture. I transfer that to a huge shallow bowl and sprinkle the whole thing with tons of crumbled blue cheese. I thinly slice the steak and shingle it on top of the salad. I pick up the plate the steak was resting on and pour all of the juice from it on top of the salad. I rub a big pinch of flaky salt between my fingers on top of the meat and sit down to the best solo meal I know.

2. **KIMCHI CHICKEN SALAD ON TOAST:** One of my favorite quick lunches. I make this chicken salad by shredding or dicing a cooked chicken breast or thigh and then finely chopping a handful of cabbage kimchi. I mix the two together with a large spoonful of mayonnaise and a splash of the liquid from the kimchi jar and season it to taste with salt and pepper. A thinly sliced scallion is nice, but it's not a deal breaker if you don't have one. Then I pile the chicken salad on toast (I like toasted challah or brioche, but use whatever you like). This is heaven with a cold beer, iced tea, or lemonade. The chicken salad is also good on rice crackers for a snack or as an hors d'oeuvre.

3. **AN EGG WITH A CHEESE SKIRT:** You know when you eat a grilled cheese and you get those crispy bits of cheese that have snuck out of the sandwich and brown in the pan? One of my favorite solo meals centers on those crispy cheese bits. I heat a large nonstick skillet slicked with olive oil and then crack an egg right into the center of the pan and sprinkle grated cheese around the egg, directly on the surface of the skillet (almost always cheddar because I'm unabashedly basic, but use whatever you want). Once the cheese is melted and browned underneath and the egg is mostly set, I slide a rubber spatula under the edges to loosen everything up and then flip the whole thing as if it were a gigantic pancake. I let the other side get a little browned (I also prefer my egg over easy rather than sunny-side up) and then slide the entire thing onto my plate. A piece of buttered toast and a little ketchup, or a few charred corn tortillas and hot sauce, and I'm good to go.

4. BROCCOLI WITH SOY SAUCE + BUTTER: Sometimes when I'm left to my own devices I like to eat slightly strange meals like an entire head of broccoli with lots of butter and soy sauce, followed by ice cream. The heart wants what the heart wants. While I wouldn't serve this meal to anyone else, when I'm making this for myself, I cut a small head of broccoli into bite-sized pieces (don't throw out that stem, just chop it up!) and place it in a saucepan with a large splash of water and sprinkle it with a big pinch of salt. I set this over high heat, bring it to a boil, cover the pot, and cook just until the broccoli is tender. I drain the water and then add a big knob of butter and a generous splash of soy sauce. Sometimes I sizzle a little minced garlic or chili garlic sauce in the butter first. I put this delicious broccoli over a steamy bowl of rice and that's that. A fried egg or a little leftover roast chicken is nice on top, but neither are needed. Broccoli is the star.

5. SPICY STRING BEAN + PEANUT STIR-FRY: In the spirit of a head of broccoli for dinner, I also love these string beans. To make them, top and tail a couple handfuls of string beans and get a skillet ripping hot. A little oil in the bottom and then in go the string beans. Don't disturb them. Let them get charred and even a little blistered on the bottom and then toss them around with a big spoonful of chili garlic sauce (such as sambal), a splash of soy sauce, a splash of water, and a large handful of roasted, salted peanuts. Once the water evaporates, they should be cooked perfectly. Great over rice or noodles or a baked sweet potato that's been split open.

6. FISH + SHRIMP IN PARCHMENT WITH SOY + BUTTER: Cooking yourself a nice fish dinner is the quickest way I know to feel very grown-up. Get yourself a single piece of fish (I like a firm white fish for this, but use whatever you like) and a few peeled and deveined shrimp (or a handful of clams). Place them in the center of a large piece of parchment paper and season lightly with salt and pepper. Mince a little ginger and thinly slice some yellow onion or a scallion and top the seafood with these aromatics. Dot the top with a tablespoon of butter and splash with about the same amount of soy sauce. Wrap the packet up tightly, place it on a sheet pan, and roast in a 400°F [200°C] oven until the seafood is cooked through, about 15 minutes. Serve with rice and vegetables or on top of some noodles. So elegant.

7. TOASTER OVEN FISH STICK TACOS: No, these don't transport you to Baja, but they're pretty great in a pinch. Cook some frozen fish sticks in your toaster oven (line that pan with foil so there's no cleanup!) until they're extra crispy. Meanwhile, char a few corn tortillas on your gas flame on your stovetop (if you don't have gas, just warm them in a hot, dry skillet) and then wrap them in a kitchen towel and let them steam amongst themselves while you thinly slice some green cabbage. Squeeze some lime over the cabbage, sprinkle with salt, and scrunch it all together with your hands. Swipe each tortilla with a little mayonnaise, top with fish sticks, the lime-y cabbage, some sliced avocado if you have a good one, and a few pickled jalapeños if you love them (I do!), and douse the tacos with hot sauce. Open a cold beer or seltzer. Enjoy.

ME GIVING MY GREAT-GRANDMOTHER
+ HER FRIENDS A FRUIT SALAD LESSON,
NORTH MIAMI BEACH, 1988-ish

MENU SUGGESTIONS

BREAKFAST FOR YOUR FAVORITE VEGANS

Walnut "Sausage" Patties (page 166)

Sweet Potato Hash Browns (page 168)

Sled Dog Muffins (page 158)

Fresh fruit

Hot coffee + juice

POST-5K BREAKFAST

Kitchen Sink Frittata (page 171)

Yogurt with Roasted Pineapple Sauce + Toasted Coconut (page 175)

Iced coffee

EASIEST BREAKFAST ON-THE-GO

Everything Bagel Hand Pies (page 163)

Clementines

Coffee in to-go mugs

PASSOVER BREAKFAST

L-E-O Scramble (page 159)

Beatrice's Bubaleh (page 167)

Hot tea with lemon

FRIENDS WEEKEND BREAKFAST

Breakfast Nachos (page 160)

Roasted Banana + Sour Cream Waffles (page 172)

Coconut water + aspirin

JEWISH HOLIDAY LATE LUNCH

Aunt Renee's Gefilte Bites (page 190)

Mushroom + Barley Soup for Dad (page 103) or Old-School Borscht (page 111)

Rascal House Stuffed Cabbage (page 40)

Apricot + Almond Biscotti (page 208)

APRÉS SLEDDING LUNCH

Creamy Roasted Tomato + Orzo Soup (page 112)

Kale + Mushroom Pot Pie (page 24)

Pear, Polenta + Almond Cake (page 219)

SPRING BIRTHDAY LUNCH FOR GRACE

Khao Man Gai (page 92)

Carrot Pineapple Cake with Maple Cream Cheese Frosting (page 224)

LUNCH OUTSIDE ON THE WEEKEND

Sizzle Burgers (page 11)

Matchstick Carrot Salad (page 120)

Fresh salad greens with Creamy Feta + Scallion Dressing (page 147)

Any Frozen Fruit + Cornmeal Cobbler (page 214)

LUNCH TO BRING TO WORK

Zucchini, Green Olive + Feta Fritters (page 200) with Yogurt, Tahini + Parsley Sauce (page 154) and cucumbers in pita breads

Palm Springs Pearl Couscous + Citrus Salad (page 128) on the side

EARLY DINNER WITH LITTLE KIDS AT THE TABLE

Llubav's Green Spaghetti (page 3)

Almond Chicken Cutlets for Grace (page 77)

Steamed broccoli

Coconut Marble Loaf (page 217)

DINNER FOR TWO ON THE COUCH

My Mother-in-Law's Brunswick Stew (page 114)

Hot rolls

Cold beer

ALL GRILLED DINNER

Arayes with Yogurt Sauce (page 20)

June's Corn Salad (page 122, grill the corn instead of boiling it)

Grilled peppers + eggplant drizzled with Easy Salsa Verde (page 150)

Card Night Ginger Cookies (page 206) made into ice cream sandwiches

VEGAN THANKSGIVING

White Bean + Pimentón Dip (page 186) with vegetables + crackers

Roasted Cauliflower Soup with Turmeric Croutons (page 108, make with vegetable stock)

Shiitake + Pumpkin Biryani (page 72)

Hasselback Carrots with Pimentón + Roasted Lemon (page 134, skip the yogurt)

Large green salad with Go-to Dressing (page 146)

Blueberry Crumble (page 212, use vegan butter)

EASY HOLIDAY MEAL

Honeyed Apricots with Cream Cheese + Pistachios (page 188)

Roast Chicken with Onion Gravy (page 90)

Braised Red Cabbage + Green Apples (page 136)

Sweet + Spicy Mashed Sweet Potatoes (page 135)

Steamed peas

Card Night Ginger Cookies (page 206)

Pumpkin + Honey Pie (page 213)

YOUR BOSS IS COMING TO DINNER

Sheet Pan Lamb Meatballs with Sweet + Sour Eggplant (page 46)

Basmati rice with Lemon, Mint + Almond Relish (page 154) mixed into it

Matchstick Carrot Salad (page 120)

Pear, Polenta + Almond Cake (page 219) with soft whipped cream

YOU ARE THE BOSS AND YOUR EMPLOYEES ARE COMING TO DINNER

Romaine with Parmesan + Peppercorn Dressing (page 146)

Stewed Chicken with Sour Cream + Chive Dumplings (page 94)

Grace's Green Beans with Garlic + Tomatoes (page 131)

Banana + Chocolate Chip Layer Cake (page 226)

A CARE PACKAGE FOR SOMEONE GOING THROUGH SOMETHING

Caribbean Pelau with Kidney Beans + Spinach (page 56)

Italian Sausage, Farro + Tomato Stew (page 116)

A jar of Go-to Dressing (page 146)

Card Night Ginger Cookies (page 206)

A GREAT COCKTAIL PARTY

Jennie's Sorrel (page 203) with mix-ins (seltzer, tequila, sparkling wine, etc.)

Aunt Renee's Gefilte Bites (page 190)

Spinach + Potato Bites (page 194)

Sweet + Salty Sesame Peanuts (page 192)

Pork + Pineapple Toothpicks (page 197)

Lemon Ricotta Cupcakes (page 218)

LISTS OF VEGETARIAN, VEGAN, DAIRY/EGG-FREE + GLUTEN-FREE RECIPES

ALL OF THE VEGETARIAN RECIPES

Llubav's Green Spaghetti (page 3)

Sesame Rice Bowls with Tofu, Quickles + Peanut Sauce (skip the fish sauce) (page 6)

Kale + Mushroom Pot Pie (page 24)

Vegetarian Muffulettas with Pickled Iceberg (page 26)

Ratatouille + Ricotta Baked Pasta (page 28)

Best Vegan Chili (page 50)

Black Bean + Corn Tamale Pie (page 52)

Caribbean Pelau with Kidney Beans + Spinach (page 56)

Stewy Escarole + White Beans with Fennel + Lemon (page 57)

More-Vegetable-than-Rice Fried Rice (page 58)

Carrot + Chickpea Korma (page 61)

Best Black Beans with Avocado Salad (page 62)

Stewed Chickpeas with Peppers + Zucchini (page 66)

Roasted Cauliflower + Red Cabbage Tacos (page 70)

Garlic + Sesame Noodles with Mushrooms + Broccolini (page 71)

Shiitake + Pumpkin Biryani (page 72)

Triple Carrot Soup (make with vegetable stock) (page 100)

Jody's French Lentil + Kale Stew (make with vegetable stock) (page 102)

Mushroom + Barley Soup for Dad (make with vegetable stock) (page 103)

Roasted Cauliflower Soup with Turmeric Croutons (make with vegetable stock) (page 108)

Roasted Onion Soup (make with vegetable stock) (page 110)

Creamy Roasted Tomato + Orzo Soup (make with vegetable stock) (page 112)

Matchstick Carrot Salad (page 120)

June's Corn Salad (page 122)

Asparagus + Snap Peas with Peanuts + Basil (skip the fish sauce) (page 123)

Potato Salad by Request (page 127)

Palm Springs Pearl Couscous + Citrus Salad (page 128)

Grace's Green Beans with Garlic + Tomatoes (page 131)

Hasselback Carrots with Pimentón + Roasted Lemon (page 134)

Sweet + Spicy Mashed Sweet Potatoes (page 135)

Braised Red Cabbage + Green Apples (page 136)

White Pizza–Style Kale (page 139)

Cheesy Ranch Grits (page 140)

Go-to Dressing (page 146)

Parmesan + Peppercorn Dressing (page 146)

Creamy Feta + Scallion Dressing (page 147)

Creamy Miso + Cashew Dressing (page 149)

Lemon, Poppy Seed + Yogurt Dressing (page 149)

Easy Salsa Verde (page 150)

Jalapeño Vinaigrette (page 152)

Cherry + Allspice Sauce (page 153)

Yogurt, Tahini + Parsley Sauce (page 154)

Lemon, Mint + Almond Relish (page 154)

Roasted Pepper + Corn Relish (page 155)

Sled Dog Muffins (page 158)

Breakfast Nachos (page 160)

Everything Bagel Hand Pies (page 163)

Walnut "Sausage" Patties (page 166)

Beatrice's Bubaleh (page 167)

Sweet Potato Hash Browns (page 168)

Roasted Banana + Sour Cream Waffles (page 172)

ALL OF THE VEGAN RECIPES

Pear, Polenta + Almond Cake
(page 219)

Granola (page 235)

Spiced Nuts (page 235)

Coconut Macaroons (page 235)

Miniature Egg White Frittatas
(page 236)

Blender Hollandaise (page 236)

Lemon Curd (page 236)

Buttermilk + Honey Pudding
(page 239)

Buttermilk Soft Serve (page 239)

Buttermilk Chicken (page 240)

Cold Blue Cheese Salad with
Hot Grilled Steak (page 243)

Kimchi Chicken Salad on Toast
(use gluten-free toast!)
(page 243)

An Egg with a Cheese Skirt
(page 243)

Broccoli with Soy Sauce + Butter
(use gluten-free soy sauce)
(page 244)

Spicy String Bean + Peanut Stir-Fry
(use gluten-free soy sauce)
(page 244)

Fish + Shrimp in Parchment
with Soy + Butter
(use gluten-free soy sauce)
(page 244)

HOPE IN THE WINDOW, 2020

ACKNOWLEDGMENTS

FIRST AND FOREMOST, thank you to my wife, Grace, my puzzle piece. Her support comes in many forms including (but not limited to): listening to every bad book title idea I've ever had, telling me in the most compassionate way to get over myself when I most need to hear that, and testing every single recipe in this book, many more than once. This book is so much more reliable, approachable, and foolproof because of her efforts. Grace: thank you, thank you, thank you, I love you.

Thank you to Melina Hammer for saying yes, and for being such a thoughtful, thorough, energetic, and warm collaborator. Thank you also to Jim Lafferty for his support throughout our very unusual shoot. I'm happy we're all neighbors. Thank you to Roger, Tanya, Erin, and Sam for getting your photo taken for the book. And thank you to my parents and in-laws for helping to dig up so many great family photos. Thank you to Winnie Au for making the cover so special, and thanks to Alex Schaefer for the extra support.

Thank you to Kari Stuart. I've lost count of how many books you've helped me create and I'm so grateful for your support. And thank you to Cat Shook for keeping things in order and all of the other kind folks at ICM who help me get my work into the world.

Thank you to the folks at Harper Wave for giving me a new place to call home and making it such a fun one. Thank you to Julie Will for being such a kind and flexible editor and just such a nice person. Thank you to Karen Rinaldi for being in the room and saying yes, thank you to Yelena Nesbit and Brian Perrin for getting the word out and to Sophia Lauriello and Penny Makras for their support. Thank you to Leah Carlson-Stanisic for making it all look so great and personal and thank you to Caroline Johnson for designing the cover. Thank you to Emma Kupor and Lydia Weaver for keeping lots of ducks in a row. And Jonathan Burnham, I'm so grateful you enjoy my meatball recipes.

Thank you to my friends, family, neighbors, and friends-of-friends who tested recipes for me and provided such valuable feedback along the way: Monica Bastian, Laura Bollin, Elaine Bonney (who went above and beyond), Cleo Brock-Abraham, Melissa Chan, Chelsea Cole, Kirsten Collins, Lisa Congdon + Clay Williams, Steph Dietz, Sara Gray, Anne Heinreich, Elena Howells, Estyn Hulbert, Kelli Kehler, Kate Levy, Emily Maletz Pagliarulo, Allison Marsh, Amelia Lang, Lizzy Oates, Mckenzie Raley, Rebecca Ringquist, Dave Roberts + Alana Blum, Kathy Rodenhouse, Eliz Roser, Adi Spiegler, Kari Stuart, Paige Thomas, Doug + Rochelle Turshen (who sent photos at every step), Kait Turshen, Natasha Warner, Roger Weiss, Renee Wilkinson, and Rachel Winard.

Thank you to Caro Lange for reading through the manuscript and offering her smart, insightful feedback.

Thank you to my professional community. Working in and around cookbooks for the last fifteen years (˙˙˙ wow!) has introduced me to some remarkable people. Thanks especially to every member of Equity at the Table and every single person who's talked to me on *Keep Calm and Cook On*.

Thank you to every independent bookstore, librarian, professor, after-school program director, and teacher who has championed my work. You connect the dots for so many of us.

Thank you to my friends near and far. And a special shout-out to my Card Night crew, Amelia, Cleo, and Lizzy. I love growing up with you three and everyone who comes with you.

Thank you to Tanya and the 30 Minutes of Everything® community for providing regular doses of strength and laughter (and distraction from thinking about recipes).

Thank you to Linda, my therapist, who helped me work through so many things over the course of making this book.

Thank you to the crews and clients at Angel Food East for inspiring so much of what, and why, I cook.

Thank you to Long Season Farm, Tributary Farm, Damn Good Honey, and all the other folks in our area who keep us so well-fed no matter what's going on in the world and who keep me so inspired as a cookbook author. Thank you to Sam and Erin and everyone at the Kingston YMCA Farm Project for letting me get my hands dirty with you all and teaching me so much more about where food comes from.

Thank you to my family, most especially to Mom, Dad, Ben, Kait, and Remy. Thank you to Jennie for always teaching me that "family" can be defined in so many different ways. Thank you to Grace's family, especially my in-laws, Elaine and Chris, for making me feel so welcome for all of these years. And to our girls, Hope and Winky, I love you so much. Turk, we miss you.

And last but certainly not least, thank you to every person who has ever bought one of my books (including this one! thank YOU!), cooked one of my recipes, listened to a podcast episode, showed up to an event, gifted my work, read a piece I wrote, shared something about one of these experiences on social media, and more. Food has helped me realize how huge the world is, but also how small it can feel. Thank you all for being a part of mine and for welcoming me into yours.

INDEX

Page numbers in *italics* refer to illustrations.

ABOUT THE AUTHOR (ME!)

JULIA TURSHEN is the bestselling author of *Now & Again* (Amazon's Best Cookbook of 2018, an NPR "Great Read"), *Feed the Resistance* (Eater's Best Cookbook of 2017), and *Small Victories* (named one of the Best Cookbooks of 2016 by the *New York Times* and NPR). She also hosts the IACP-nominated podcast "Keep Calm and Cook On." She has coauthored numerous cookbooks and has written for the *New York Times*, the *Washington Post*, the *Wall Street Journal*, *Vogue*, *Bon Appétit*, *Food & Wine*, and more. Epicurious has called her one of the 100 Greatest Home Cooks of All Time and the *New York Times* has described her "at the forefront of the new generation of authentic, approachable authors." She sits on the Kitchen Cabinet Advisory Board for the Smithsonian's National Museum of American History and is the founder of Equity At The Table, an inclusive digital directory of women and non-binary individuals in food. She lives in the Hudson Valley with her wife and their dogs.